POETRY RE

AUTUMN 2000 VOLUME
EDITOR PETER FORE
PRODUCTION JANET PH
ADVERTISING LISA RO

GW01396270

CONTENTS

Illustrations by Gerald Mangan

POETRY REVIEW
SUBSCRIPTIONS
Four issues including postage:

UK individuals £27
Overseas individuals £35
(all overseas delivery is by airmail)
USA individuals $56

Libraries, schools and institutions:
UK £35
Overseas £42
USA $66

Single issue £6.95 + 50p p&p (UK)

Sterling and US dollar payments only.
Eurocheques, Visa and Mastercard payments are acceptable.

Bookshop distribution:
Signature
Telephone 0161 834 8767

Design by Philip Lewis
Cover by Janet Phillips

Typeset by Poetry Review.

Printed by Grillford Ltd at
26 Peverel Drive, Bletchley,
Milton Keynes MK1 1QZ
Telephone: 01908 644123

POETRY REVIEW is the magazine of the Poetry Society. It is published quarterly and issued free to members of the Poetry Society. Poetry Review considers submissions from non-members and members alike. To ensure reply submissions must be accompanied by an SAE or adequate International Reply coupons: Poetry Review accepts no responsibility for contributions that are not reply paid.

Founded 24 February 1909
Charity Commissioners No: 303334
© 2000

EDITORIAL AND BUSINESS ADDRESS:
22 BETTERTON STREET, LONDON WC2H 9BX

telephone   **020 7420 9880**   fax **020 7240 4818**
email   **poetryreview@poetrysoc.com** ISBN 1 900771 22 5
website   **http://www.poetrysoc.com**   ISSN 0032 2156

Funded by
THE ARTS COUNCIL OF ENGLAND

The Poetry Society is supported by
BT

READER POWER

by Peter Forbes

CHRISTOPHER REID ONCE said that he had never seen anyone reading a poetry book on the Underground. At the time I would have said the same, but it's not true any more. You do sometimes see someone reading poetry on the Tube, and the chances are it will be one of the *Nation's Favourite* series. Indeed, it happened the day before I started writing this. The success of these books is even more astonishing than the phenomenon of Hughes's Ovid and Heaney's *Beowulf* becoming bestsellers. When the series was launched, the editor, Daisy Goodwin, had to battle against considerable scepticism within the BBC. Now they release several titles a year, yet when the Poll of The Nation's Favourite Twentieth-Century Poems was conducted in 1996 no book was produced at the time because it was felt that even if Kipling *et al* sold, twentieth-century poetry would not. This year that has been triumphantly disproved.

The success of the *Nation's Favourite* series is the most dramatic thing to have happened in poetry for years and yet it isn't much talked about in the places where poetry is hotly debated. It's taken for granted now as a rather vulgar phenomenon that can't have much to do with the business of creating the taste by which contemporary poets can be enjoyed. This is wrong. All previous successful crowd-pleasing anthologies have mined the same seam of pre-1900 favourites. But Daisy Goodwin, who invented the idea, is thoroughly contemporary poetry savvy and managed to smuggle in good helpings of current poetry. The range of twentieth-century poetry known to those who don't normally read much poetry is thus broader than it was.

It is worth trying to identify just why the *Nation's Favourites* are such a success. Likely factors include: the use of polls, which short-circuited the critics and *parti-pris* poets and created the People's Choice at just the time when "The People's ." became a stock formulation; the fact that it was BBC1 and Griff Rhys Jones who put the show on the box and all in a relentlessly joky entertainment context, rather than dressed in the solemn robes of high art; a good deal of overlap between the volumes. What people seem to need to get to like poetry is a familiarisation process rather than a parade of new work.

Another prong in the advance of reader power has been the rise of online bookselling. This now has about six per cent of the market and is growing rapidly, which means that whereas in the beginning sales were heavily weighted in favor of computer books, they now represent a good cross section of the market. And of course Amazon produces regularly updated charts – actually the only useful poetry chart in existence. More importantly for this issue, Amazon also features customer reviews. Much of the comment on Amazon is refreshingly acute and free from fashionable cant. Several of the reviewers here were recruited from the Amazon site.

And then there are the reading groups. In the beginning was *Birdsong*. Word of mouth made it a bestseller, then came *Captain Corelli*, Kate Atkinson's *Behind the Scenes at the Museum*. The heady whiff of reader power encouraged people to set up reading groups. Canny publishers and literary promoters like Waterstone's and the Orange Prize for Fiction, Harper Collins, and Random House, started producing lists and other material for the groups.

Poetry has not so far figured strongly in reading groups but of course it is well suited – the commitment to read a slim volume before the next session not being too onerous a burden. We have reviews from members of reading groups here and one from someone who could claim to be *Poetry Review's* reader in residence *avant la lettre*: Matt Holland, organiser of the Swindon Literary Festival, leader of two reading groups, and organiser of the residential courses at Lower Shaw Farm. Besides the online reviewers and the reading group members, there is a smattering of regulars. The reviews thus run the gamut of styles, from Sue Wade's sceptical but ultimately convinced what's-in-this-for-the real world look at Alison Brackenbury to David Wheatley's informed view of William Empson. There are many ways of writing about poetry. Excepting the tired and formulaic, most have some validity.

The Larkin – Duffy Line

BY JUSTIN QUINN

IT IS OFTEN thought that the emergence of Carol Ann Duffy in the 1980s indicates how much has changed in British poetry since World War II. The Irish surname, born in Glasgow, educated in Liverpool, leftist politics, didn't attend Oxbridge, and of course open lesbianism – all of these aspects touch on important new developments not only in poetry but in British society in general. It is not surprising then that with the imaginative ability to work these elements into her poetry she has enjoyed much success in the last decade. The biting wit and dramatic flare were vehicles with which to address some of the central preoccupations of British people in this period. The accepted critical picture is one of a break with the past, a break, as Sean O'Brien has it in *The Deregulated Muse* (1998), into a new "variousness". He continues: "It seems at the moment that poetically *anything* is possible, though not necessarily desirable, and that form is undergoing a radical inspection". More particularly, in his advocacy of Duffy, he is at pains to show how pioneering her work is as it breaks from the previous Larkin-dominated generation. After all, Larkin was the man who called left-leaning universities "superfluous nest[s] of treason-soaked layabouts"; who sighed contentedly about his neighbourhood: "Not many niggers around here I'm happy to say. Except the Paki next door"; who said of the Arts Council Literature Advisory panel: "I agree with you it should all be scrapped. No subsidies for Gay Sweatshirt or the Runcorn Socialist Workers Peoples Poetry Workshop. Or wogs like Salmagundi [Salman Rushdie] or whatever his name is"; and finally who said of Margaret Thatcher: "What a superb creature she is – right and beautiful". If Larkin was, as Donald Davie

> But for all the talk of New Generations, gender politics and post-colonialism, when one reads Larkin and Duffy together it becomes clear that far from being a radical break with the past, Duffy is the latest exponent of the tradition which in the twentieth century goes from Hardy to Thomas to Larkin. Of course, aspects of Duffy's brand of Britishness would have made Larkin foam at the mouth...

wrote in 1972, "for good or ill the effective unofficial laureate of post-1945 England", then it simply must be the case that the success of a poet like Carol Ann Duffy marks a sea change.

Or so one might think. But for all the talk of New Generations, gender politics and post-colonialism, when one reads Larkin and Duffy together it becomes clear that far from being a radical break with the past, Duffy is the latest exponent of the tradition which in the twentieth century goes from Hardy to Thomas to Larkin. Of course, aspects of Duffy's brand of Britishness would have made Larkin foam at the mouth (one wonders what he would have written to Kingsley Amis about a book like *The World's Wife*), but in terms of poetic canons and styles that is a marginal matter. By this last statement, I don't wish to appear New Critical: it is precisely because Duffy has caught much of the energy of recent social change in her poetry that she is so important. Similarly, Larkin was an excellent stenographer of a time when people didn't much believe in such possibilities. Davie described Larkin's work as a "sell out" of the transformative possibilities of poetry, a "lower[ing] of sights and settl[ing] for second best", and it is precisely this aspect that has disappeared in the work of Duffy. Whereas Larkin would end poems with an elegiac panning shot, Duffy will often end with an imperative to action or vision, so that she seems to participate in, if not actually in some way to activate, social change. A large part of her rhetorical power draws from the increased political power of groups that were previously marginalised by the very social hierarchy that was so dear to Larkin. But what I wish to suggest is that for readers of poetry as opposed to students of cultural studies, such a difference is not of great importance. The shared stylistic features outweigh it, and to a great extent the terms of Duffy's engagement with politics, gender and the matter of and with England, were given to her by the Larkin tradition. The difference I sketched out above and which most commentators feel to be fundamental is essentially only a difference in verb mood.

So what exactly are those commonalities? Both Larkin and Duffy belong to what Antony Easthope in *Englishness and National Culture* (1999) calls the British empiricist tradition in poetry. According to Easthope, the presumptions of this tradition are "(1) that the subject is coherent and autonomous, (2) that discourse is in principle transparent, and (3) that reality can be experienced directly"; connected with this is the poet's attempt "to give the effect of someone 'really' speaking". Easthope compares this unfavourably with work that comes out of Modernism – the latter kind of poetry foregrounds the materiality of language ("We are forced to become aware of the text as text"), and this, he implies, should be the aim of a vital, forward-looking culture. Easthope is not so naive as to think that the "coherent and autonomous" subject of this poetry is untouched by the experiences it relates: it does indeed undergo crises and syncopes, but these are usually brushed aside in the end as the self is shored up and affirmed in the poem's closure. As literary criticism, this is grapeshot, but it is of some use in drawing attention to Duffy's conservatism compared to other poetry that takes its lead from Modernism, for instance poets like Jorie Graham or Frank Bidart in the USA, or for that matter, poets like James Merrill and Paul Muldoon whose intense engagements with form lead them to extend its boundaries. What Edna Longley calls "Duffy's erratic formal instinct" is stanzaic organisation that owes much to Larkin but with a much loosened hold on rhyme.

But the commonalities go even deeper. The most open statement of affinity between the two poets comes in 'An Afternoon with Rhiannon' from *The Other Country* (1990):

> The night before, our host had pointed out the
>   Building
> Larkin feared. *He was right*, I said, suddenly cold
> and wanting home; cold later, too, in bed, listening
> to wind and rain whip in to the lonely, misplaced
>   town.

This refers to Larkin's poem 'The Building', which begins in awed description but quickly turns to fear:

> Higher than the handsomest hotel
> The lucent comb shows up for miles, but see,
> All round it close-ribbed streets rise and fall
> Like a great sigh out of the last century.
> The porters are scruffy; what keep drawing up
> At the entrance are not taxis; and in the hall
> As well as creepers hangs a frightening smell.

That "great sigh" is the touch Larkin was so expert at: a lugubrious scene is transformed with expansive metaphor. It remains of course a moribund sigh, but the imaginative leap to it from the streets brings an element of surprise into the dull panorama. The poem ends by confirming the pathos and fear before death that the building instils:

> ... All know they are going to die.
> Not yet, perhaps not here, but in the end,
> And somewhere like this. That is what it means,
> This clean-sliced cliff; a struggle to transcend
> The thought of dying, for unless its powers
> Outbuild cathedrals nothing contravenes
> The coming dark, though crowds each evening try
>
> With wasteful, weak, propitiatory flowers.

It might seem that this poem contradicts Easthope's description of the British tradition, but at no point in the poem is the ability of the speaking subject to survey the situation shaken or threatened. It does conclude not with a celebration of the self, but rather in a confirmation of the fear and powerlessness of all selves. Nevertheless the voice that tells us this maintains its aplomb when expressing this feeling. I do not agree with Easthope that this aplomb is "Neo-Georgian" or a symptom of the culture's lack of vitality. It is rather an instance of the paradoxical ability of poetry to maintain its own rude good health in the face of moribund subject matter.

Duffy's instinctive agreement with Larkin's fear when confronted with the Building is part of a larger range of resemblances and rhymes between their poems. In the following passage, Sean O'Brien wishes to differentiate her from her male predecessors by pointing to her different take on history, but only ends up confirming her similarity:

> [S]he rarely steps back for a direct attempt on the
> long perspective by which numerous male poets,
> including Larkin, Hughes, Hill, Harrison and Dunn,

have been in their various ways concerned – and to which, as we have seen, they are all in thrall. This is not an adverse criticism of Duffy: her poems' comparative lack of interest in the world before 1945, and the resulting sense that history has "gone missing", contribute to the subtle representation of fragility and exposure which recurs in the poems.

Now Larkin was indeed interested in the world before 1945 (the most obvious example being 'MCMXIV') and Duffy for the most part isn't. But the reader ignorant of all facts about the two poets' lives might be led to believe from O'Brien's comments that they were born in the same year. Born in 1922, Larkin was interested in a turning point like 1914 for the most part because it was the immediate prehistory of his own childhood world. In the same way Duffy, who was born in 1955, and who, like Larkin, frequently employs an autobiographical persona in her poems, only stretches back to about 1945. O'Brien was born around the same time as Duffy and thus might indeed feel that a greater aura of the English past is attached to Larkin's poetry, but that has obscured from him the underlying structural resemblance. More important than the 33 years between their dates of birth is the similarity in the way they both interweave public and private history. Neither Larkin nor Duffy ever deals with the English past in as detailed a way as, say, Geoffrey Hill does in *Canaan*. Of 'An Arundel Tomb', which would seem to engage the English past directly, David Gervais comments that "I can't help myself from feeling that the poet is not interested enough in the medieval tomb for the poem to be as much of an epiphany as it would like to be... Larkin is not very interested in what the tomb has to tell about their world".

Another point arising from O'Brien's characterisation is the idea of history "gone missing". In 'Originally', Duffy brilliantly orchestrates the dislocations of her childhood (from Glasgow via Staffordshire to Liverpool) to accommodate a wider sense of such loss:

All childhood is an emigration. Some are slow,
leaving you standing, resigned, up an avenue
where no one you know stays. Others are sudden.
Your accent wrong. Corners, which seem familiar,
leading to unimagined, pebble-dashed estates,
                      big boys
eating worms and shouting words you don't
                     understand.

My parents' anxiety stirred like a loose tooth
in my head. *I want our own country*, I said.

The speaker is melancholy and aghast at the loss she has endured. Her italicised protest in the last line is at once an expression of her wish to return to her previous home, but more largely an expression of all people to return to "the other country" from which they emerged into the world. Her "parents' anxiety" is then both their worry that their move to the new city was wrong because of the effect it is having on their daughter, but also the anxiety of their own existence. In *The Other Country* as a whole Duffy prolongs this sense of ghostly origins and makes it echo through many different contexts, including the love poems that come later, most wonderfully in 'Survivor':

For some time now, at the curve of my mind,
I have longed to embrace my brother, my sister,
                    myself,
when we were seven years old. It is making me ill.

Also my first love, who was fifteen, Leeds, I know
it is thirty years, but when I remember him now
I can feel his wet, young face in my hands, melting
snow, my empty hands. This is bereavement.

Or I spend the weekend in bed, dozing, lounging
in the past. Why has this happened? I mime
the gone years where I lived. I want them back.

My lover rises and plunges above me, not knowing
I have hidden myself in my heart, where I rock
and weep for what has been stolen, lost. Please.
It is like an earthquake and no one to tell.

The break in communication between the two lovers recalls Larkin's 'Talking in Bed' and the country that Duffy's speaker has survived is described with exactitude in his 'Home Is So Sad'. That land has become a precinct of the imagination:

                It stays as it was left,
Shaped to the comfort of the last to go
As if to win them back. Instead, bereft
Of anyone to please, it withers so...

But perhaps Larkin's finest expression of the lost country of childhood is 'I Remember, I Remember'. "Coming up England by a different line", the speaker finds the train stopped in Coventry, where he was born, but has difficulty orienting himself, and then:

> ... A whistle went:
> Things moved. I sat back, staring at my boots.
> "Was that," my friend smiled, "where you 'have your
> roots'?"
> No, only where my childhood was unspent,
> I wanted to retort, just where I started ...

The question put to the speaker here is very close to that put to the speaker in Duffy's 'Originally'. After the emigrations of childhood: "Now, *Where do you come from?* / strangers ask. *Originally?* And I hesitate". Duffy's 'Hometown' also covers much of the same ground as 'I Remember, I Remember'. Origin is difficult for both poets.

But more largely, Larkin is preoccupied if not with an England that has "gone missing", but which is "going missing". The most outright and most unconvincing statement of this sentiment is of course 'Going, Going', where Larkin evokes an ersatz England of "The shadows, the meadows, the lanes, / The guildhalls, the carved choirs". Much more persuasive in this respect is 'The Whitsun Weddings'. To hear Easthope tell it, this poem is an occasion of jingoistic pomp. According to him it makes a "claim to national universality [sic]", but only as imperceptive a reader as he could miss that it was the disappearance of national unity that is the subject of the poem. The poem's much vaunted final epiphany is not shared publicly (Easthope, in a fit of pique, even surmises that most of the newly weds were copulating on the train before it pulled into London) – it is restricted to the private awareness of the speaker. The elegiac tone of the poem conveys that this is the last we are probably going to see of such old English traditions.

Larkin plays with the idea of "another country" haunting one's mind, and even the necessity of it, in 'The Importance of Elsewhere'. Living in Ireland, the speaker is lonely and constantly reminded that his home is across the water. Rather than discomfiting him, paradoxically, it makes him feel that his human situation has been established with the utmost clarity. There is relief at this, but:

> Living in England has no such excuse:
> These are my customs and establishments
> It would be much more serious to refuse.
> Here no elsewhere underwrites my existence.

But of course in other poems set only in England, Larkin finds other phases of difference – his lovelessness, childlessness, increasing industrialisation – with which to make him feel apart and foreign in his own country. These are the terms passed on to Duffy.

One of the most important devices Duffy uses in *The Other Country* is collage, not within poems themselves, but between them. With this technique a poem like 'Following Francis', about becoming a disciple of the saint, becomes an oblique way to chart the "conversion" from heterosexuality to lesbianism, which is another of the book's concerns (it is followed immediately by 'Survivor'). Several poems of childhood nostalgia open the book and their elegiac tone could not be more different from a poem like 'Poet for Our Times':

> I write the headlines for a Daily Paper.
> It's just a knack one's born with all-right-Squire.
> You do not have to be an educator,
> just bang the words down like they're screaming *Fire!*
> CECIL-KEAYS ROW SHOCK TELLS EYETIE
> WAITER.
> ENGLAND FAN CALLS WHINGEING FROG A
> LIAR.
> ...
> The poems of the decade... Stuff 'em! Gotcha!
> The instant tits and bottom line of art.

Duffy is aware of the linguistic force wielded by this leader-writer, and she uses this kind of ventriloquism again in 'Fraud' and 'Mrs Faust'. Her mimicry indicts rather than validates the speakers, as they parade their obnoxiousness before us in technicolor. The leader-writer is one of Larkin's "cast of crooks and tarts", who in 1972 he said would take over England in a short while; and the carefully timed vulgarity of Duffy's final line here recalls Larkin's use of the same device in poems like 'Sunny Prestatyn' and 'Reading Habits'. But more importantly, Duffy employs the stratagem which Larkin uses to such effect in 'Naturally the Foundation Will Bear Your Expenses' and 'Posterity' – that of ventriloquising the voice of a speaker the poet despises.

The pairing off of poems could go on (Larkin's 'Posterity', Duffy's 'Biographer'; 'Ambulances', 'November'; 'Mr Bleaney', 'Room', etc.), and by drawing out these parallels I don't wish to suggest that Duffy is derivative, rather I wish to show to what degree she is working within and not against the tradition that Larkin represents. She has extended it in her poems of eros, for instance, 'Sleeping' and 'Steam', and in poems of the underside of such passions, such as 'Adultery'. The voice in this last poem is probably the one most critics are thinking of when they differentiate her from Larkin. In it she achieves a demotic white heat which is nowhere to be found in his *Collected Poems*:

So write the script – illness and debt,
a ring thrown away in a garden
no moon can heal, your own words
commuting to bile in your mouth, terror –

and all for the same thing twice. And all
for the same thing twice. You did it.
What. Didn't you. Fuck. Fuck. No. That was
the wrong verb. This is only an abstract noun.

Larkin was incapable of the kind of exchange that takes place in the last two lines here, and we should be grateful to Duffy for plumbing the depths of a relationship and the demotic with such fidelity. To be part of a tradition means to extend it.

Also, some readers would draw my attention back to 'An Afternoon with Rhiannon' pointing out that I omitted the upbeat ending that has the Building transformed in the eyes of the small girl of the title. She proclaims: "*I like buildings!*" , daylight floods through the poem, and in the end, "the shy town smiles". But Duffy takes most of the poem to move away from her instinctive sympathy with Larkin, and even towards the end her description of the "poet's slow, appalling, ticking night" carries a good deal more weight than the sweetness and light of the sonnet's concluding couplet. Perhaps this girl will write poems beyond this tradition, but Duffy stands with Larkin and to see her poetry in the way recent criticism has is to fundamentally misread it.

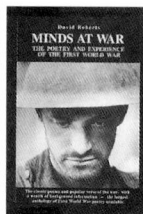

TWO POEMS BY MICHAEL DONAGHY
REGARDING OUR LATE CORRESPONDENCE

Often I'll begin to write to you
and find I'm simply copying the plot,
that glass machine that dictates what we do.
   And often I'll be chalking up a cue,
clocking each ball rolling towards its slot
in that web of vectors
            – and I'm *crap* –

   But it's my balance makes me miss my shot;
balancing the angle of my aim
against the random factors of the nap,
   or point of impact, say, or force, or weight,
or the chance of having missed the game
or having turned up pissed,
          an hour late.

   But like I said, I'm crap at games.
I know. *We* know we can't finesse what's been.
we only have that instant of our skill,
   to squint across a field of abstract green,
or print *forgive me* in unbroken script,
sharpening the focus of our will
on making what comes next be
        what we mean...

   which is where my aim has always slipped,
As often, in the night, I freeze mid dream.
Just before I wake and lose the drift,
   a soft *clack* startles me, I turn towards you,
a million miniature pistons shift
the spindly camshaft of a vast machine
beneath the rumbling as the last balls drop.
   As, often, I'll begin to write to you,
        and stop.

5:00/5:10/5:15

We shared a dream beneath
a dream-beneath-a-dream.
Our tears became a storm
that washed away our names
and our voices blended with the rain's.
Whatever does the singing sang
about, and then away, the pain
of having been
one creature torn in two.

Then whatever does the waking
woke, or dreamt it woke, to share
our dream-beneath-a-dream
before the primed alarm could tear
us back to me and you.

This is no dream: It's 5:15.
I wake. I pack. Before I go
I'll press my ear against your back –
a hostage at a wall – to hear
one beat. No. two beats fall.

ALAN DIXON
THE NAME CRANESBILL

The name cranesbill
Would not have come about
Had there been no more cranes,
But now we have only the cranesbill
And those cranes
Not like the cranesbill.

How conjugal the cranes must have been,
Their heads in pairs
Like heads on one neck,
Or two necks twisted,
Craning upward
After the pink wedding.

ROGER McGOUGH
EVERYDAY ECLIPSES

The hamburger flipped across the face of the bun
The frisbee winning the race against its own shadow
The cricket ball dropping for six in front of the church clock
On a golden plate, a host of communion wafers
The brown contact lens sliding across the blue iris
The palming of small change
Everyday eclipses.

Out of the frying pan, the tossed pancake orbits the Chinese lampshade
The water bucket echoing down into the well...
The black, snookering the cueball against the green baize
The winning putt on the eighteenth
The tiddlywink twinking toward the tiddlycup
Everyday eclipses.

Neck and neck in the hot air balloon race
Holding up her sign, the lollipop lady blots out the belisha beacon
The foaming tankard thumped onto the beermat
The plug into the plughole
In the fruit bowl, the orange rolls in front of the peach
Every day eclipses another day.

Goodbye bald patch, Hello Yarmulke
A sombrero tossed into the bullring
Leading the parade, the big bass drum, we hear cymbals but cannot see them
One eclipse eclipses another eclipse.

To the cold, white face, the oxygen mask
But too late
One death eclipses another death.

The baby's head, the mother's breast
The open O of the mouth seeking the warm O of the nipple
One birth eclipses another birth
Everyday eclipses.

MAURICE RIORDAN
THE SPHERE

Why bother with words? Geometry existed before the Creation – Kepler

When to do so – when to imagine the world
as a sphere hanging in the heavens – meant
you belonged to a sect, Eratosthenes measured
the earth's circumference: a number that lived
through burnings and mayhem, through the centuries-long
recessions, and reached Columbus as a whisper
(who, had he trusted it, wouldn't have sailed).

It helped that Eratosthenes was Librarian
at Alexandria, that Alexandria stood
on the Nile delta, that the Nile made a straight line
due south across the sand to Syene
where – the librarian read – the noonday sun
at midsummer cast no shadow but blazed
into the well-shaft and lit it like a torch

– as if nature and history had contrived
a vast Euclidean figure, the Mouseion
(and himself) at one of its points: the basis
for a calculation that spread the map
beyond the dreams of emperors but which proved,
when the earth was viewed like a water-ball
spinning calmly in space, almost true.

Did Eratosthenes worship sun and river?
Fear the marsh elf, the gaseous bogle?
When he looked out across the harbour and saw
the water curve, the lighthouse tilt; as he stretched
and oiled the scrolls, when year after year he unrolled
the nibbled theorems, did he simply wonder?
Or see in them a shadowy signature?

TWO POEMS BY RUTH SHARMAN
THE TRAVANCORE EVENING BROWN

As if by naming it I were naming you,
who've learnt to mimic withered leaves
and fade into the shadows; as if a name
could pin down all that's fragile
and sounds could recreate the patterns
of who you are and what you know,

I'm raiding your store, eager to know
why this name means so much to you,
learning about his violet patterns
and underwings like withered leaves,
her browns a reflection too fragile
for the evening of her name.

That day you mentioned the name
in passing, wanting me to know
how they dance at dusk, as fragile
as shadows, it could have been you
who was dancing, like the bracken leaves
in the wind making silver patterns,

and so I'm weaving patterns
with these thoughts about a name,
building a bridge of shadows and leaves,
making links all too fragile,
since there's no other way I know
to reach out and touch what touches you.

It's this butterfly that touches you,
and those weaving courtship patterns
few of us will ever know,
since the place that shares its name
shelters an existence as fragile
as the memory of light on leaves;

so before it vanishes like leaves,
and names no longer mean as much to you,
I'm gathering in memories as fragile
as leaf shadows or the invisible patterns
of larksong, repeating a name
that dances to a tune only you can know

– as if through leaves and shadow patterns
and things as fragile as a name
I could know for certain how to reach you.

LEAFBOAT

And each time we pushed one
into the darkness like a leafboat

weighted with petals
on the Ganges at dusk,

we'd ask for a gentle wind to guide
our handmade hull

into the silence of the mother water
and carry the candle of life

safely downstream
for each daughter or son,

and we'd stand on the bank
watching for signs, searching

for our light in the darkness,
or for roses on the river,

knowing how many flames by now
had flickered and died.

PENELOPE SHUTTLE
CHOOSING, SENDING

Choosing a leaf,
a shiver, a grief,

sending it from hand to hand
across the world,

not a masterpiece,
not the only perfect leaf,

more like a moon
not asking to be the only moon

or be told –
I like you enormously

Just my leaf,
my shiver, my grief,

journeying
as far as it may,

call it your own

CONNIE BENSLEY
AMONG THE DEAD MEN

Wisps of mist are tenuous
round this solid boat-like shape
but the crashings are not waves.

We move intricately,
each feeding a dark orifice
from a hoarded, gleaming cache.

A man beside me, grey-moustached, limping,
wishes he too could be recycled:
"I'd drop myself in, no sweat".

We are the reflective ones:
not for us the showy swing
of the ship-christener;

not for us the winners'
hubristic champagne-showers,
the profligate, heady waste.

We know about quiet change
and renewal. Or at least
we are making a gesture towards it.

VERNON SCANNELL

REMEMBERING THE DEAD AT WADI AKARIT

The Millennium slithers to its close. A haggard December
damages the daylight; the bruised sky lours,
then darkness drapes the town though, in the Square,
the patient clock denies that this is night.

The old man gazes through an upstairs window-pane
over polished tiles and lemon lozenges of light
to where the town becomes an orange-tinted glow
against the sky. Thunder mutters like an afterthought.

This rumbling, though, reminds his mouth and throat
of a sharp, blue bitter-sweetness in stunned air
and slips a still-fresh picture in the window-frame,
replacing the orange-smeared darkness there.

He sees the shapes of rock, the sand and rubble
on which, at unshaven dawn, the bodies sprawl
or lie with unpurposed and tidy decorum,
all neat in battle-order and KD uniform.

Disposed in their scattered dozens like fragments
of a smashed whole, each human particle
is almost identical, rhyming in shape and pigment,
all, in their mute eloquence, oddly beautiful.

As the sun strengthens, a faint sweet feculence spreads.
Dark birds wheel and soar. Fresh light applies
a maquillage of ochre and red. Furtive needs
and greeds begin to plunder the submissive dead.

The old man's eyelids flutter. He shakes his head.
The picture holds, then fades and slowly disappears
with cordite-breath and the pungent sweetness of the dead.
What stays is the shade of the unforgiving years.

DANNIE ABSE
YOU HAVE BEEN THERE

There is, indoors, one place
that is always deserted
like a dentist's waiting room
on a Sunday afternoon.

No flowers in the vases,
no candles in the candlesticks.

You have been there.

The mirror on the wall
reflects another mirror.
A spider scuttles across the floor,
a fly shivers on the window pane.

Once you asked,
"Whose ordinances? What statutes?"
You say you have forgotten
– and you have forgotten.

Outside then, as now,
the generality of rain.
Intermittent cars saying "Hush"
and then again "Hush",
the sound of brush on stone.

Every One a Winner

Sue Wade exerts her reader power

ALISON BRACKENBURY
After Beethoven
Carcanet £6.95
ISBN 1 85754 454 4

WHY AM I, Sue Wade, an unknown, unprofessional lover of language from near Swindon writing about Alison Brackenbury's new collection *After Beethoven*? The editor of *Poetry Review* has discovered that fashionable genre, the "ladies' reading group" and as a long standing member of two groups, I have been asked by Peter Forbes to represent their views on Alison Brackenbury's new work. As my first aside (we are rather tangential in our group) we would wince at the term "fashionable" on three counts: a) we have been reading together, some of us, for 20 years; b) rural Wiltshire doesn't succour fashion slaves; c) we have men in our group. So, sorry Alison, you won't get the formal, logical analysis you deserve but more an enthusiast's rating.

But having unearthed us (I thought Alison would like that rural metaphor) – and it is known there are at least 350 and possibly 50,000 reading groups in the country (yes, there is a university study of them!) – your editor sensibly thought to access them and spread what Richard Dawkins and Susan Blackmore would call poetry "memes". There is big buying power out there but more importantly warm appreciation of the wordsmith's skills.

Being typical of our group of 18 (we are librarians, tennis coaches, ex-teachers, radiographers, garden designers, school inspectors, magistrates and school governors – but preferring to be facilitators and enablers to husbands, children and the local community – thank you Theodore Zeldin) I am delighted to be a conduit to our world and particularly to be asked to review Alison Brackenbury with whom we would certainly identify. Our greatest pleasure is to recommend writers to friends and family. If we feel a writer is intelligent and intelligible, creates mood and a sense of place, finds appropriate and innovative metaphor, connects with the universal, feels relevant, and has a sparkling or mellifluous style, we would come up with a "recom-mended". Let's see how we might rate Alison's new work *After Beethoven*.

Being back-packers, V.S.O.s and international business class travellers, we would all appreciate her wide geographic range from third world, far-flung Hanoi through sophisticated London parties to rural rides and back to domestic hearth. Her historical interest (a particular trigger for Alison) would stimulate and intrigue us. It reaches back to Roman poets, Elizabeth of York through Ben Jonson and Shakespeare and arrives in the present with Princess Diana's funeral. But it would be her emotional range to which we would most relate. These are mature landscapes, and with an age range of 35 –83 in our group we would understand her reactions to death, sense her bitterness at betrayal in relationships, share her regret at wasted opportunity, feel her disgust at hypocrisy, feel weighed down by her burdens of secrecy in fleeting and unsatisfactory meetings, fret with her at the frustrations of domestic chains and suffer her anxieties of parental concern. We would appreciate the stoic resolution to continue and find a meaningful future. They are not joyful themes and humour is not Alison's tool or medium but her handling of these grown-up themes is intelligent and controlled. She leaves a sense of possibilities and regeneration after emotional trauma and partings.

Her title poem 'After Beethoven' chillingly incorporates these themes. Alison says it was triggered by "a chance hearing on the radio of the story of a mysterious lady who turned up to Beethoven's funeral". She has that great skill of all good writers to place you in a period, create a scene and imagine emotions. In her own words, "I try to hear in history not its truth but its music", and in this case the jangle of rejection by a lover who "struck her with silence", the secrecy of "a veiled lady", the hypocrisy of "with their false rings", yet the forward momentum and release of "Her feet, in their small boots, broke through the snow / Softer, and faster, like a young girl dancing". Death may be a "snuffing out of a candle" but she captures the universal mood of listening to "the echo he became". By history then, Alison is fired up.

But it is the natural world where Alison excels.

We are a rural (not a green) lot down here in Aldbourne and we would empathise with her observation and use of nature to trigger philosophic thought. We would comment on her presumed acceptance, if not choice of, cover for this collection. Eileen Agar's *Figures in a Garden*, is brilliantly appropriate for her sombre themes. Although dominated by its dark, strong tree (or are they pathways and metaphoric choices?) with distracting or tantalising fruits and death masks, it still offers sunshine beyond. The proliferation of words like "woods", "grass", "tree", "corn", "fields", "ivy", "marigolds", "bluebells", "wild garlic", "anenomes", "buttercups", "badgers", "gulls", "rooks", "sparrows", "flies", "deer", "larks", "snails", "wind", "rain", "ice", "snow", "fog", "mist" and "frost" does not denote sentimentality – they are rather the inspiration for mood and reflection. 'At Last' is a very tangible poem recalling a fleeting encounter with a badger which we would recognise as a metaphor for that delightful experience of being taken unexpectedly, if only briefly, into a completely different world ("That's the charm", I can hear a member of the class say), only to be "recalled" to ordinary life. We live much engaged with life but our literature classes give us that brief interlude to stand back and observe, as poets do. Alison's nature metaphors and references

would please us enormously.

We would be interested in the presence of "you" in her poems. It seems to be a constant reference point. Is it the present "you" of a husband or lover? Is it a past "you" of a parent or dead loved one? Is it the poet herself? Is it one or many "you's"? – "You call it heartless", "Beside the wood, you said", "Drowsed, strange, you say"... It is a universal feeling of referring, conferring or even deferring to others. Alison has captured it.

She frequently uses open ended, somewhat Socratic questioning and thankfully avoids "political correctness". Death is again addressed in 'The Princess Funeral' with the question "How can we be remembered?" comparing the life of a famous person with the life of an inconspicuous caterpillar. It is mature. We would find this relevant.

Narrative style, (particularly in 'A Short Story') lyricism and loose rhyme which is easy on the ear – an echo rather than a din – make her writing accessible and mellifluous. She composes a cathartic cadence.

The big test then. Would we recommend? A definite and enthusiastic YES. We are better at enthusiasm than formal reviews, but we are in the real world, and know that enthusiasm wins converts and keeps followers. We like it when everyone wins.

Bridge of Crane

By Phil Ramage

PAUL MARIANI

**The Broken Tower –
The Life of Hart Crane**

Norton £12.50
ISBN 0 393 32041 3

The Complete Poems of Hart Crane

Ed. Marc Simon
Centennial Edition
Liveright/Norton £19.95
ISBN 0 87140 656 X

IN 1932 HART CRANE climbed over the railings of the SS Orizaba and threw himself into the sea. It was the last, inevitable, yet unpredictable gesture the thirt-two-year-old poet would make. He was *en route* from Mexico, where he had achieved drunken notoriety in place of the epic poetry he had envisaged, virtually being bundled out of the country to save the reputation of the Guggenheim Foundation who had sponsored the Mexican adventure. He was going back home, to America, the country which had inspired his greatest work yet which to him was further testament to his lack of achievement – the home of creative highs and financial lows. He was accompanied on this journey by his only heterosexual lover, taken in Mexico as his life really began to spiral out of control, in what could be seen as a last-ditch attempt to impose some conventionality onto his existence, but which may have hastened his end.

The sea is a powerful image within Crane's work and it is ironic, yet somehow fitting that he should have chosen this way to depart from his troubled world. By joining the murky depths he was fusing the metaphor with his life, even to the extent of being searched for by the sailors who he himself would have searched out for sexual encounters in docks and ports around New York. It can be cynically seen as a way of achieving notoriety and continued attention, of ensuring the focus on his slim body of work. There really was no way that Hart Crane was ever going to get old.

Paul Mariani has written an impressive biography of this frustrating, frustrated genius. It is a very detailed, extremely readable account of the man who promised so much yet found it difficult consistently to come up with the goods. The sense of a man who lets down all around him and who continually lets himself down in the pursuit of inspiration is so clearly depicted by Mariani – at times Crane is pathetic, scrounging and thoroughly unlikable and yet it is obvious that Mariani is writing this as a labour of love to both the man's work and his extraordinary life. Feelings which, after finishing this book, the reader is likely to share. For what Mariani has done here is in itself extraordinary: he has written a biography so vividly entertaining that an interest in Crane's poetry is largely insignificant and yet he has also provided those who are interested in the poetry with a superb key with which to unlock a lot of the mysteries of Crane's work.

Reading the poetry of Hart Crane is no undemanding task. His densely metaphorical style was a result of writing and rewriting over and over again – working for years on his most celebrated poetic sequence 'The Bridge' and thrilling and puzzling contemporaries in equal measure. Some of those who championed him then disowned him, a betrayal which added to the poet's disillusionment. He was a poet out of his time, apolitical in the time of fervent politicisation of the arts, backward looking in a progressive era, enthused by alcohol in the time of Prohibition and with a rampant lust for sailors at a time when blackmail could have destroyed the little reputation he had.

But what of the poetry itself? An initial reading of much of Crane's work triggers a response at the unconscious level as his rich metaphor and allusive language seeps in. Closer analysis sometimes brings forth explanations and greater understanding – but not always. It is times such as these where Mariani's

analysis of the life helps. Crane's references were often intensely personal and can only be revealed by an understanding of his life's events – his cultural sweep can encompass Whitman, Emily Dickinson, Pocohontas and Isadora Duncan all within a few lines – once again Mariani is able to put these references into perspective for the baffled reader.

But there is great reward in reading the Centennial Edition of Crane's work. From the haunting, gently nostalgic 'My Grandmother's Love Letters' – his first significant poem (and his first pay cheque) which has slight cadences for me of D. H. Lawrence's 'Piano' – to the extraordinary homage to love and the sea in 'Voyages' which was the highlight of his first collection 'White Buildings' – there is much to appreciate. His *raison d'être* – 'The Bridge' sequence, often compared to Eliot's 'The Waste Land', with more than a passing nod to Walt Whitman, is complex, rewarding, frustrating and yet so impressive. With this work Crane achieved the poem for which he had been searching, a poem that would, he believed, put him alongside the greatest of American poets.

In the *Complete Poems* we are provided with *The White Buildings* collection and 'The Bridge' sequence – together with his less successful 'Key West' work, in which he could sense the inspiration slipping away – together with uncollected, unpublished work and fragments of which some (namely 'Porphyro in Akron', 'March' and the romantic observation 'Episode of Hands') suggest that there would have been more great works to come. Being submerged in the work of Hart Crane is a rich and rewarding experiene made even more pleasurable with Paul Mariani as guide.

Phil Ramage writes:

Up until last year I was working as a Headteacher in a London Primary School and despite a passionate interest in children's literature, there was little time for reading other than Government documents! I have managed to escape to run a Guest House in Brighton and having reclaimed my life am able to find more time to re-experience literature. I've put the occasional review on Amazon.com when I feel passionately about a book and find it a valuable way of reading the opinions of others. I have found myself reading things I've waited years to read and am loving every minute of it.

Politovsky's Pen

By Matt Barnard

DOUGLAS DUNN

The Donkey's Ears

Faber & Faber £8.99

ISBN 0 571 20426 0

THE DONKEY'S EARS is the kind of book that makes books worth having and which Faber are so good at producing. It's just the right size and shape with a bold red cover that's got a precise yellow drawing of a labelled cross-section of a battle-ship on the front. The font and size of the print inside are pleasing, as are the cream pages which I find much easier on the eye than the harsh white of a publisher such as Carcanet.

It also has a strange and interesting title, and the notes on the back explaining that it is based on the letters Flag Engineer Politovsky sent to his wife Sophie as the ship he was on "led a Russian fleet around the world to its destruction at the battle of Tsushima in May 1905", did what they are intended to do and whetted my appetite. It seems a particularly poignant story-line in the light of the loss of the Russian submarine, the *Kursk*. Added to all that, it is written in very digestible four-line stanzas with many numbered sections to each of the nine parts into which the book is divided.

There are certain passages which certainly live up to its promise, but largely I was disappointed. The iambic pentameter, abba-rhymed stanzas provide a melodic and testing form, but are not overly restrictive; occasionally the form is broken where it seems convenient. The metre for the most part is handled expertly, though there are a few lines which appear not to scan, such as the line in the tenth section of part seven, "Tonight, for seen breath and the belled drench", which would only work if "belled" is pronounced with two syllables (which I suppose it might be as I have still not worked out what it means).

My favourite passage is the last section of part four where the narrator is describing the ship docked in Nossi-Be off Madagascar, which includes a visceral description of a working vessel at rest:

...a stillness such
As no one other than an engineer

Can understand, someone like me, whose ear
Makes sense of sleeping boilers, warm to the
touch ...

This is not the only passage that seems to work, but there are too many in between that don't. The reason I felt let down is that although the metre is strong and flexible, over and over again the content seems to have been dictated by the need to fill a line or find a word to rhyme. The admiral doesn't like his subordinates proposing discussion and he's said to despise "Whoever's mischief dared even to propose it". This sounds wordy; surely the line should read "whoever dared even to propose it", and the reason it does not seems to be because it would mean the line was missing a stress.

Another line reads "And dandy's lost much of his scornful, smug, / arrogant patriotism", in which three adjectives are used where one would be much better, in order that "smug" is in the right place to rhyme with the earlier line ending "shrug". The consequence of this looseness is that the reader loses his faith in the writer, and also that Dunn doesn't seem to have control over the poem. It goes off on tangents which don't seem to add anything, or gets repetitive and re-examines the same idea with the result that the narrative seems flat. The reason for this problem, I think, doesn't lie with any lack of talent on Dunn's part, but is a problem with the voice in which he has chosen to write the poem.

The book is based on the letters the real Politovsky sent his wife, but its conceit is that Politovsky is an amateur poet consciously writing those letters in verse. At one point Politovsky asks "What's this I do? A diary or a poem? / Or letters to you?", but the problem is, as a reader, I'm not sure that Dunn knows the answer. The verse doesn't read at all like letters to a loved one, they have none of the idiosyncrasies that letters normally have, none of the unexplained references.

The occasional nod to "my dear" sounds purely rhetorical, and the artifice is taken to the point where the narrator describes the feeling of reading letters from his wife as if it wasn't his wife he was writing to, "... I couldn't get my fill / Of your letters, while those words you misspell ... / Excite me, make you real again ..." This means that instead of creating a fleshed-out rounded character and the real sense of someone at sea writing back to a loved one left at home, the voice sounds like a vehicle to discuss such themes as imperial overstretch, professional versus aristocratic value systems and the modernisation of warfare.

In the author's notes Dunn reveals that at times "I felt that I had become my narrator, and I didn't much care for the experience", and unfortunately for the reader precisely the opposite seems true. As someone once said, "metre is a great bullshit detector". If you don't get the voice right, the form finds you out; conversely, when you do get the voice right everything seems to fall into place as if it was always meant to be there. Having said all that, *The Donkey's Ears* did pass what I consider to be the most basic test of any literature by worming its way into my unconscious. The night before writing this, I dreamt of Politovsky and his ill-fated voyage.

Matt Barnard writes:

As with many people, it was an inspirational English teacher at school who first got me interested in reading and attempting to write poetry, and I have continued the struggle, on and off, since then. My work as a journalist has meant that I've written on a variety of subjects, from the debate over metre and free verse for the *Times* to the environmental implications of grouse shooting for the *Guardian*. While my interest in poetry and literature has helped my journalistic career through an increased sensitivity to the use of words, the discipline of writing regularly for demanding newspaper editors has helped me appreciate the importance of a rigorous and professional attitude to whatever form of writing one approaches, which I think the best poets bring to their work.

A Life in Poems

By Jane Hardy

FLEUR ADCOCK

Selected Poems: 1960–2000

Bloodaxe, £10.95
ISBN 1 85224 530 1

READING FLEUR ADCOCK'S *Selected Poems: 1960–2000* produces the same kind of pleasure as reading autobiography or even a very personal novel. There are characters, narrative, a self is revealed. And as Sally Vincent discovered in her recent interview with the poet (*The Guardian*, July 29), Fleur Adcock rather likes the finality of this volume's title. It does sum things up. So here is her emotional life charted from when her children were small ('For Andrew') to when they are grown and travelling ('On a Son Returned to New Zealand', which opens gloriously: "He is my green branch growing in a far plantation"). Here are depression and writer's block ('Dry Spell'). Here are the relationships good and bad, including 'Advice to a Discarded Lover' and the witty 'Against Coupling' ("I write in praise of the solitary act") and there seems something also solitary – but not masturbatory – about Adcock's art. You sense she has discarded unnecessary verbiage to achieve the clear line, the spare observation, very much as she has discarded the wrong man.

But the art of Fleur Adcock should not be taken at face value, with an autobiography's veracity and dates. Her verbal texture(s) and way with straight-forward language alter things, the way water changes shapes. As she writes at the end of 'A Message': "Read between these lines".

One of the reasons Fleur Adcock is so anthologised is that she's very good. Another is that her tone is the tone of the end of the twentieth century. She does irony, for example, as well as anybody. She is self-aware, uses our speech-patterns, and it is almost impossible for a reviewer to sum her up without reaching for adjectives such as "wry", "laconic", etc. As she says, wryly, in 'Poem Ended by a Death', after chastising herself for a cheap opener as she imagines nurses wiping her kisses and tears off the body: "This is my laconic style". Sometimes the title itself is almost enough, as in 'The Genius of Surrey', although the poem helps flesh out the absurdity of something so explosive in such a manicured county. The ending says it all: "As for Surrey's genius / that was found to be for the suburban".

A well-known Adcock, poem, 'For a Five-year-old', illustrates this ability to speak for our time. Ostensibly a personal poem about a mother called to see her son's surprise visitor climbing up the window sill "after a night of rain", Adcock broadens it out. She explores the little boy's trust that his mother will know the right thing to do:

I explain
that it would be unkind to leave it there; it might
crawl to the floor; we must take care

that no one squash it.

The poet describes her son carrying the snail outside to eat a daffodil. So far, so pastoral, almost an "Aaah!" poem, albeit in spare language. But the mood changes as she examines the ambiguity in the "kind of faith" underpinning the experience. Her child's world contains a necessarily benevolent parent, and his behaviour is shaped by her diktats. Yet she, who recommends kindness to snails, has trapped mice, killed things, "betrayed your closest relatives", and is in reality an unreliable dictator. The poem ends:

> But that is how things are: I am your mother
> and we are kind to snails.

Here the brisk statement of fact changes gear into something reminiscent of, say, Henry Reed's 'Today We Have Naming of Parts'. Similarly, in 'Comment', from the same collection, Adcock nails the illusions we live by. Here it's a question of the big one, romance. She lists unlikely occurrences – her son pretending to like vermouth, her cat eating cheese. Equally implausible is the sight of her and her partner, like some latter-day Adam and Eve, walking in gardens "hand in hand / underneath the summer trees". The pointed comment undercuts her seductive rhyme-scheme. Like another New Zealander, Katherine Mansfield, who was famously said to convey the snail beneath the leaf, Fleur Adcock always spots the underside of life.

Andrew Motion has perceptively noted her ability to write about bedroom activity – not just sex (at which she is superb in poetic terms, see the first verse of 'Prelude') but also dreams, the internal life. He is right. She has written marvellous poems about dreams, including 'Mornings After', which recounts nightmares so gross she disowns them. And her mode is internalising, personal, again like the century just gone. In her affectionate memorial to James K. Baxter, she lists the good times and her impressions in decent Shakespearean iambics, before admitting she is false-footed by his death and the need for grief:

> But I can't alter
> this message to a dirge; the public attitude
> Isn't my style: I write in simple gratitude.

Yet although hers is a private world, Fleur Adcock does engage with politics and society. She writes caustically on the Greenhouse Effect, and in 'The Farm', a moving poem about the premature death of Fiona Lodge, exposes the authorities' cover-up over the leukaemia clusters around nuclear installations:

> And no matter what the authorities said
> about there being no risk at all from the installations
>   at Calder Hall,
> buckets of radiation spread, and people are dead.

The childish rhyme underlines the grown-up hypocrisy and wickedness. You can almost see a hovering '60s banner about the personal being political. Adcock is green, unsurprisingly for someone who clearly loves and brilliantly details the natural world. In 'Happiness', which she sums up in a neat bathetic simile as like "being supported on warm porridge", she lists the aspects of the outside world which make her happy. "Gazing at this: may-blossom, bluebells, robin, / the tennis players through the trees". She often uses this quasi-Imagist technique of matching feelings to an external detail. This happens humorously in the next poem in the book, 'Coupling', where she observes a pair of crane flies having sex by jump-starting each other from behind. She adds: "It looks easy enough. Let's try it".

Just as Keats didn't simply write odes, Fleur Adcock does not exclusively write short, laconic observations on life. There are impressive longer poems in the books, such as 'Gas', in which she imagines almost the end of the world, and the 'Soho Hospital for Women', not to mention her brief party political ones, which must work well in performance. I particularly relished 'A Political Kiss', about kissing John Prescott, and 'Apology', which asks, rhetorically as it turns out, "Can it be that I was unfair / to Tony Blair?"

Where is she in the pantheon? Adcock is "Establishment" enough to own an OBE. Her writing bears comparison with the best Americans such as Adrienne Rich who also make the domestic count for more than the obvious. Fleur Adcock is also master of the short story poem. I am thinking of poems such as 'A Day in October'. Here her gift for layering circumstance and feeling works like a story. She charts her visit to the National Gallery; research on a book detailing the atrocities of nuclear war; and a Middle Eastern spat possibly involving people she knows. Her final line, "And I do not write political poems", contains its contradiction. She implies it's more serious than that. Adcock's poetry will last because she combines clear diction with wit and a real sense of the darkness underneath. In 'From the Demolition Zone', Adcock defines literature, and therefore poetry, as a tough healer. She addresses "clear-eyed literature, diagnostician", imploring it to be "our nurse and our paramedic". In the end, literature provides salvation as a means of articulating our real subversive selves. It says the things "we're afraid of saying / In case they hear us".

What the reader hears is whispers of disaster. From 'The Soho Hospital of Women' and its account of women facing death with fortitude to 'Last Song', where the world's gone "skew-whiff" through our abuse, Adcock has the medieval and earlier, classical sense of time passing.

Recently, Fleur Adcock has taken up genealogy. In the penultimate section, *Looking Back*, she renders the moustachioed men, heroic women of previous generations in verse. Naturally, there are good lines and lives, but I prefer her poems on her current family. 'The Chiffonier', for example, uses discussion of a potential heirloom to tease out the mother-daughter relationship. It's a kind of letter and very affecting, as if the poet has thrown off her customary detachment. "I have to write this now, while you're still here / I want my mother, not her chiffonier". There is also little detachment in the poems about grandchildren.

In the *Guardian* interview, Adcock seemed to be toying with the idea of retirement. She has even written a poem called 'The Ex-Poet'. Some of the final poems here hint as much. 'Goodbye', for example, which marks the end of summer and the collection and concludes, "The chestnut blossoms are dead / The gates close early. What wanted to be said is said". Reading between the lines, I hope she's having us on.

Jane Hardy writes:

I have written poetry since the age of seven. As Fiction & Poetry Editor of *SHE* magazine in the '80s, I published Keats alongside Vikram Seth, Wendy Cope and readers' poems. As half of 'poetry unplugged', a group formed with northern Irish poet Michael Conaghan, I organize poetry events in Kent. 'Poetry is often called the new rock'n'roll or whatever image journalists find comes to hand. In fact, as a genre, it has a secret life far more important than that. I know from working on *SHE* that in any given street in the country, someone, somewhere, will be writing poetry. It may be therapy, it may not be good formally, but he/she is paying tribute to the way poetic form enables people to articulate important emotions and ideas.

Troubadors, Song and Dance

By Kwame Dawes

JEAN "BINTA" BREEZE
The Arrival of Brighteye
Bloodaxe, £7.95
ISBN 1 85224 538 7

PATIENCE AGBABI

Transformatrix
Payback Press £7.99
ISBN 0 86241 941 7

JEAN "BINTA" BREEZE'S *The Arrival of Brighteye* is a lively collection of verse that confirms Breeze's wonderful sense of wit and her capacity to write poems that resonate in sound and intelligence. What she achieves in these poems is a linguistic triumph that reveals what can be done with work that straddles two strong language traditions. Breeze has no apprehensions about situating herself as an inheritor of at least two language traditions – English and nation language with its Jamaican and Trinidadian incarnations – in her work. She dances happily along a continuum of idiom and lexicon and creates a language that is exciting for all it carries of the dialogue between the traditions and the culture that give rise to these languages.

It is worthwhile putting the achievement into perspective. Breeze, often seen as a performance poet, is precisely that: a poet committed to all the implications of performance. She shows that the truest performer is one who understands the medium she is using and the demands of the space in which she is performing. In *The Arrival of Brighteye*, her stage is the page, and she leaps at the opportunity to show the capacity of poetry to take glorious flight off the page, while encouraging us to enjoy the reflective lyricism of work that appears in books.

The collection is anchored by a series of sensual meditations on sexuality and discovery that some times are rooted in childhood memory and other times reveal a sexually unabashed voice. But sex is constantly the source for a joyous kind of amusement and pleasure. Sex is not fraught with undue trauma even though its pitfalls are there. For Breeze, it is an absurd pleasure, and she engages in exploring this absurdity in some of the most sensuous poems. In 'Flowering' we see how a girl's coming into the startling sense of her menstrual cycle transforms the playfulness of childhood sexual games:

When she finally let me in, there, flowering on her
　　　　　　　　　　　　　　　　white
Panties, a bright red hibiscus, newly printed, damp.
I made it home through the storm, frightened of
　　　　　　　　　　　　　　　　blood.

It is the nuance with which motive and action and then shock play in this poem – irony is the glue, a certain playfulness. The girl-persona is the aggressor, she wants to touch, to enjoy the sexual play with her girlfriend, then she sees the sign of menstruation – a shocking sign that fills her with dread both of the act of sexual play which is riddled with taboo, but of the foreboding sense that she too might be so wounded by time.

The collection moves from small poems, terse observations in both Jamaican dialect and conventional English, to a movement of extended pieces that show Breeze's ability to manage large issues and her ability to tell a tale. She is a splendid story

teller. In the title poem of the sequence, she tells the poignant story of migration – the loss, the sense of shame, but the cycle of families trying to make sense of their constant movement. At the end, Brighteye is the mother now, struggling to make sense of her feelings of homelessness despite the fact that she has lived in London for most of her life. She becomes her grandmother. The effect is touching. In 'Ole Warrior', Breeze takes on the voice of a middle-aged man who once was quite a woman's man. He is over the hill and what Breeze achieves is a poignant telling of this man's failing with such empathy and charm. She allows him one last articulation of dignity at the end of the poem – a truly Calypso moment:

So I ain't coming out today – no play, boy
I ain't coming out today
ole warrior mus retire
young blood mus find dem way
is a dance dat de devil design
when yuh young, he ain't give yuh no sign
so ah weaving home unsteady
Ah trying to whistle an rhyme
an ah reading bout growing tomato
in dis damp and wintry clime
An ah praying dat wen ah finally end
dis journey dat some call life
de fires of hell will claim mi again
cause ah gwine fuck de devil wife.

In this Breeze shows her facility with the Trinidadian language – the rhythms slightly different from Jamaican tones. Breeze is a careful listener – she understands how to capture these tonal differences.

Unquestionably, however, the most impressive of the poems is a piece in which the politics of gender, themes of madness and the role of the actor as creator and artist are combined, the poem 'Playing Messiah'. Breeze's sense of timing is impeccable here, but what is impressive is the quality of confession tempered by wit and irony. Shango and the Christian God come into uneasy contact – Breeze will not resolve this encounter. The poem is a gem.

Jean Breeze may have been just the poet that influenced the performance sensibility of Patience Agbabi. They share a few things; both have published their work in books, both are well respected on the performance stage, and both enjoy the business of not indulging in questions about their positions as performers. Of course, tonally, they differ. Breeze writes with an assured sense of maturity – a sense that she really cares little about the act of confession and self-revelation; hers is a less contained feminist sensibility. There is a sexuality that rests comfortably on the reader – nothing tightly held about it.

Agbabi in her new collection, *Transformatrix*, is less candid about her confessions and chooses to explore her emotive ideas through a series of poems that are tensely contained in form and the masking of personae. She is exceptionally gifted at using conventional forms, particularly the sestinas that she experiments with in the sequence 'Seven Sisters'. Here she takes on a challenge: to make seven poems of varied tone and style using not merely the sestina as a form, but using the same end words for all the poems. It is an impressive *tour de force* in neo-formalism, but fortunately, she does not leave us merely impressed with her handling of form. There are some poems in the sequence that are, quite simply, wonderfully rendered and felt: in 'The Earth Mother' we see Agbabi's instincts for the well-turned phrase and the use of surprise:

Old Woman woke and saw her baby Boy was girl
and being wise, gave praise and raised this girl-child
to chop the wood and mend the roof. By dark
the three would eat hot pottage. Girl and Boy
sat side by side, Old Woman at the end
remembering the time
that first weekend, when the pot bubbled wild thyme
and a child lit up the dark
bowl of her belly, the girl-child she named Boy.

Her sonnets, three of which end the book, are equally reflective of her care for making her rhymes interesting, and managing her thoughts in relatively strict form. There is something to be said for the achievement as it sometimes allows Agbabi a funky use of rhyme and line breaks that seems even more alive and boundary-breaking than the idea of a sonnet would suggest:

At twelve I learnt about The Fall,
had rough-cut daydreams based on original sin,
nightmares about the swarm of thin-
lipped, foul-mouthed, crab apple-
masticating girls who'd chase me full
throttle; me, slipping on wet leaves, a heroine
in a black-and-white cliché; them, buzzing on
                                                    nicotine

and the sap of French kisses. I hated big school

Her rhymes are clever, subtle and effective in containing the tumble of images and ideas in something that creates the right kind of tension that the best poems need – the sense of something waiting to explode.

Transformatrix is a collection full of so many pleasures because Agbabi in this collection is constantly willing to experiment not just with forms, but with various moods, various tones, various airs, from the urban funk of the drug-induced madness of 'Ajax' to the staid elegy for a veteran of World War II in 'Poppies and Fresh Red Ribbons'. Note her effective management of sentiment here, despite the slightly off note of "starched with memory" – a flaw we can bear:

Arthur is remembering
Joe speaking blood. He's singing
hymn number one in silence
resonant as shell shock. "Once
you kill a man, you kill twice:
war's intimate sacrifice...
the living mimic the dead".
Memories of Joe's naked
torso, ...

Arthur has loved without him
almost sixty years. Women
press his clothes. His uniform
is starched with memory. Warm
firm hands shake his, some shaking.
The congregation rise, sing
remembrance. Then men embrace
their sixty seconds of peace.

Agbabi likes to tinker and toy with language, with meter and with sound. Her emotional range is strong, but it is never indulgent – almost to a fault. Yet her restraint is a trope in itself, a masking that suggests something disturbing lurking beneath the well-built structure of the poems. This collection shows that Agbabi has grown tremendously as a poet since her debut *R.A.W.* – a collection that glimmered on the surface but lacked the depth of idea and discipline that we see in *Transformatrix*. Yet, in all of this Agbabi has not lost the quality of troubadour and song and dance woman that she carries as a performance poet – and it is this quality in the work of these two gifted poets, that we come to appreciate above everything else.

TWO POEMS BY JOHN FULLER
MOSAÏQUE MACARONIQUE

Interlocking circles seek
A teasing labyrinthine plan
Au travers le Basilique,
Un pavé cailloutis romane.

Galets lisses de St. Pierre,
Blancs et noirs, ils s'entremêlent
And we ourselves are walking there,
Treading the shapes of Heaven and Hell.

Dim penitential voices bless
The soaring vaults with F in alt,
Mais sous les pieds de nos faiblesses
Sont cailloux polis de basalte.

Austère Mosé et St. Pierre
Se rencontrent en mosaïque,
Stone on stone established where
The law itself is a mystique.

A grown cathedral can be seen
As something larger than a cairn.
Ses carrés rouges comme nougatine
Coupés des volcans de l'Auvergne.

Parfois dans le Basilique
Le basilic comme hypnotiste:
Mountains are where the guilty seek
Interrogation of the Beast.

The walls delight in the grotesque;
God has a righteous chase in view.
Démembrements animent les fresques;
La voûte dévoile un Absolu.

Le Samedi chez le Basilique
Parfum de basilic, tomates.
Stalls along the pavement reek
Of all that haunts the human heart.

Every earthly thing we risk
Eternity to smell just once:
Odeur de la jeune odalisque,
Le sensualité d'encens.

MADAME FURET

Madame Furet on her whirlwind visit
        Has much to tell,
Banging at cupboards that will not open
        (Just as well),
Nosing at bags, fruit-stones, fruit-rind,
        Ends of bread,
Lifting her head to a table, diving
        Under a bed:
"When you may well in a year or two
        Be much vexed
To wonder further than the breath
        That is your next
And not impossibly your last,
        Remember me
Who live entirely at such moments,
        Free and unfree
By virtue of my breeding close
        To hopelessness,
That hedge-home where comfort has
        No known address.
I give you one brave look, as though
        You were a god
Whose only carelessness, to leave
        Crumbs where you trod,
Were too painful a puzzle for solving,
        As though square caves
Were hunger's heaven, defining the space
        In which the slaves
Of cornerless Nature are translated
        To emperors,
And the emptiness a mystery
        Daunting to us
But truly a required adventure
        A threshold crossed
In despite of danger to my kind
        And the sky lost.

But, shadowless, you do not move.
    In your eye
Is a surprise of recognition.
    Let me pass by
Before you find me quite at home.
    Be still in surprise:
Give me time to be gone
    Or otherwise
Yourself turn from our encounter.
    You will have time
To judge, with humour if you will,
    My little crime."
Bow-legged, one wave from ear to tail,
    She scampers past
With a panic skitter on the tiles,
    Moving fast
For green and safety. And the cease of speech.

ELEANOR COOKE
CAPITAL

It is reported that the House Sparrow, Passer domesticus, *is virtually extinct in Central London.*

A woman is buying a scarf, delicate as dreams.
She takes from her handbag
eleven wells,
fifty-three children,
seventy-eight spades: and seeds – so many seeds
you could feed a million sparrows
ready to drop off their perches
unnoted except by God.
"Rubbish", the woman says. "There are no sparrows,
and as for God,
he's one of the disappeared".

I'll paint his name on a placard;
chant it –
    His name shall not be spoken:
commission a portrait –
    His face shall not be seen:
I'll stand outside heaven's embassy

and demand to know
who has taken him,
where they have put his body.

An official comes out
and explains that he is not authorised
to disclose the whereabouts of God.
As for the sparrows,
he attributes their disappearance
to the acute shortage of grubs
to feed the chicks. He hands me a paper
with the ISBN number
of the relevant HMSO leaflet.

The woman walks by,
dropping the till receipt into the gutter
and fastening the scarf round her neck
with a slip knot.
"I'm hanging God", she says.
"It's nothing personal. I'm campaigning for
the re-introduction of capital punishment".

BRIAN HENRY
THAT'S HOW I SPIN

When tempted toward anger I think of Shakespeare –
How he makes me angry, his manner.

As if virtue could survive so many centuries.
As if knowledge could be portrayed.

Let's discuss a one who matters,
The boulevard of lost causes behind us, betrayed.

How to conclude passion has not been spent
Beyond our reach, our pasts the lust without the grace?

An impasse most neglectful of what
We most cherish. When what we most cherish

(Ourselves) conflicts with what we most hate –
[see above] – drama ensues.

The uses of drama are many, as are
The uses for drama. When annihilation

By malevolent deity was the chief cause of death
Among children, the written word existed

Only in books. Drama then was as daily
A part of life as weeping.

Now that the glazed word has replaced the written word,
Children are, in general, safe from their god.

Yet death by exercise destroys countless
Otherwise healthy citizens, as does death by implosion:

The skull, that ordinarily resilient covering,
Suddenly deflates, like a lung

Punctured by the poke of a rib,
Like an ancient jar placed, with malice, on the sun:

The jar, rather than cracking, hisses,
Or seems to hiss

As the heat divests it of all that oxygen.

SIMON RAE
LOCAL

The cigarette disappears
in the cave of his palm.
That's his bar-stool
you're sitting on

but the grizzly-bear arm
doesn't reach out
and fling you aside
like a laundry bag

or a sack of straw.
Instead he waves
a permissive paw
on which he's inscribed

the usual half
of the usual stuff
about Love and Hate
and his name, twice,

and settles down
to the evening shift
in which he'll shift
a pint per stone

to the tune of twenty,
his belly gently
rising and falling
like a broad-beamed tug

at ease at its mooring.
He's a big man
and it's worth reflecting
he doesn't need you

to remind him of it
by coolly inspecting
the bar-room floor
or the stippled ceiling

like a claims assessor
after a fire
supposedly caused
by faulty wiring.

But don't overdo it
by staring too hard
at the bridge of his nose
untidily scarred

in a brush with the sleeve
of a broken glass
or the sole of a boot
stirrupped with steel.

His breath feels hot
in the hair of your nape.
He's used to being
 a chicken-neck's snap

from a serious charge
but a man who could break
the back of a horse
with a trampoline bounce

or shift an upright
into the street
via the open window
without raising a sweat

has nothing to prove
and you're no threat.
You're his friend,
his companion in arms,

so enjoy the joke
but don't laugh too loud
and don't try to cap it.
Stay one of the crowd

(a crowd of one)
and you won't regret it.
A word to the wise:
there's a thin line

and a golden rule
for the likes of you
with the likes of him.
It's something to do

with a weather-vane whim
and the perception of status.
Airs and graces
are usually surplus

to any requirements.
There's a lot of brunt
that you'd have to bear
as a la-di-da cunt

if it came to that.
But don't pretend
on the other hand
to be what you're not.

It's a delicate balance
and what you risk
is the weighty opinion
of a ring-heavy fist,

a tear-gas salad
of finely chopped onion
served on the edge
of the nearest table

and a ketchup spoor
zig-zagging its way
all the way from the bar
to the tap-room door...

ROS BARBER
PRONOUN

You never say her name; I never ask.
Pronouns walk us far

through the late night confessions,
next morning reassessments.

Her unsaid name blows about us
uncatchable as willowherb fluff

and as light
and as ready to seed;

and as sleeplessness
mottles the pigments

in my skin
her name spells itself in melanin:

a soft, emergent tattoo.
Once, before I started loving you,

I rang you at home.
A female voice on the answerphone

paired up your names like Jacks
like silver cruets

like evening gloves
smoothing them out at the elbows.

Hers was there, pressed against yours
and I thought of two corpses

discovered embracing
in the ruins of a fallen building,

having loved each other
to death.

ALEX WEBB
THE GARDEN AT GIVERNY

The Americans vied for position
On the *Pont Japonais*, taking photos –
So familiar, this composition:
Water, wisteria and willows.

Still wonderful, of course, but these gardens
Were meant to be private, yet we all hope –
The groups who walk these paths in their dozens –
He'll speak to us alone, the old myope.

So I duck away from some Taiwanese
And find a spot where I can briefly crouch,
Bamboo-hidden, through half-closed eyes reprise
The mauve water lilies, and then debouch.

J.B. Priestley once said the very hours
Had shortened since the century began;
Could the light, too that danced on these flowers
Have weakened in the intervening span?

Perhaps – but the reason these canvases
Still fascinate is something that's withstood:
The beauty that resists time's trespasses
Is the light we remember from childhood.

And that is what brings them here, the coaches,
The mums and dads, the big soft girls in jeans,
Fleeing the pallid light that encroaches
Once you're drawing pay, or over your teens.

This is where he caught it, the play of light:
Water, air merging in a dazzling haze;
Turn-of-century afternoons, whose sight
Can still remind us of our own lost days.

But behind the lilies lies something dark,
Not of painting, but laboratory:
The dance of atoms, electrons and quark;
Nothing is real; matter is energy –

Then I think of your contemporary,
Another man with long beard and white hair
Who split not an atom but a world, and
Said, "All that is solid, melts into air".

ROSE FLINT
SELKIES

In caves and crannies, under thrift and sea-campion
the women are seeking their lost children.
Round and round every rock they go
dabbing their butterfly nets at shadows –
    the nets are torn full of holes
      and the women's harsh calls pierce
    the wind and water silence.

The children are in the water
under the wave where the women can't look.
They are swimming like small seals,
but their mouths are open, saying O

O mouths open for milk, for lullabies, for kisses.

The women are frantic, turning and staring,
their hair flying into their eyes, their limbs
heavy as cut trees. The wind stokes them with
    one hand of compassion and one hand edged
    with the sharp silver of memory;
      the wind's shifting voice
    has all the history of whispering.

Too many bodies swimming like seals in the blue.
Small and rounded, the blue filters through
and they have no edge between water and bone
they are blue, salt, seal-baby-ghosts
on the sea's blue coil, faces small, white, bruised,
    mouths open in O
             O Mother
their eyes are brimming with salt,   blue
   spilling the ocean out of themselves.

Names never spoken become songs in the wind's speech
My Twelve-week Child, My Red-Cell, My River-child,
My Murder, My Bird-Without-Breath

O Mother Ocean   the women are beating the sea
with their torn nets and their hand's helplessness.
They weep in a clamour calling white birds
with their wings of silk who come wheeling and diving
into the baby-shoals, collecting their souls
and flying home.

      And the women go on
somehow   not turning to stone
under the sky where the seabirds gleam and weave
they go on   searching
      for the perfect comfort and fit
   of their own sealskins, hidden somewhere
      at the edge, on the shore,
in the liminal space of caves or crannies.

ANDY CROFT

THE HOUSE BEAUTIFUL

"From the place where he now stood, even to the end of the valley, the way was
all along set so full of snares, traps, gins, and nets here, and so full of pits,
pitfalls, deep holes, and shelvings" – John Bunyan

From Houghton House the sleepy plain's
   A beer-mat scene of harvest gold,
Where citizens of sleep's domain
   Wake up to find their dreams gone cold
And England sold to profiteers
   In sleepy, sleepy Bedfordshire.

Between the quarries and the bricks
   Between the landfill and the clay,
All earthly aspiration sticks
   Hungover in the light of day,
Like those who sup on Bombadier
   In sleepy, sleepy Bedfordshire.

But something in this treeless vale
    Still stirs the yeast of earth-bound schemes,
Like prelate's broth and local ale
    And chiliastic sects that dream
Of Armageddon's panacea
    In sleepy, sleepy Bedfordshire.

Between the morning star and bed
    The valley sides are strange and steep
So pilgrims lay their sleepy heads
    As in a dream and yet not sleep
And see a vision shining clear
    in sleepy, sleepy Bedfordshire.

He who would leave a tinker's cottage
    Proving dreams are not for sale
Must learn to price a mess of pottage –
    (Twelve years banged up in Bedford gaol)
For peaceful dreams come very dear
    In sleepy, sleepy Bedfordshire,

As sleepy taxi-drivers know who're called
    On midnight trips to even scores
In smack and cocaine border wars
    And end up dead to all the world;
Their progress marks the wild frontiers
    Of sleep in sleepy Bedfordshire.

And pilgrim tourists passing by
    Don't see the cracks beneath the street,
They keep their eyes upon the sky
    And not the pit beneath their feet
Who follow steps that disappear
    Up wooden hills to Bedfordshire.

While Mansoul's fast asleep in bed
    The night takes flight on cobweb wings
And crawls inside the sleeper's head
    To lay the eggs of nightmare things
That breed Diabolonian fears
    That stir in sleepy Bedfordshire.

But even sleepy English scenes
   Like this must choose to dream or wake
And know the difference between
   The two and waking help to make
The cold night's pitfalls disappear
   In sleepy, sleepy Bedfordshire.

What's lost by night's regained by day
   As morning washes Mansoul clean,
The sun comes up once more to slay
   The monsters of the night's ravine
And shows the sun-lit way shine clear
   On hills that lead from Bedfordshire.

JOHN HARTLEY WILLIAMS
THE MACHINE
POEM IN FIVE SENTENCES

Of course the operation of chance makes us sad –
it's a mechanism of such intricacy, such febrile, whizzing purpose,
undoing logic, pulling rugs from under feet
with gossamer claws that grab & whisk away
the carpets, those who stand upon them, & vanish everything
so swiftly into the black hole of fate, that frankly
you feel disappointed & then annoyed & then quite melancholy
that life should contain such expeditious little grabbers,
not to mention the mill-wheels of crunching Derbyshire stone
between which everything is judiciously pulverised before being
blown into the atmosphere to become the stars
you stand there ruefully gazing up at
from the temporarily too-solid ground.

This juggernaut was invented by a Frenchman,
by name Jacques le Sourd,
(or Jack the Deaf, as we would say in English)
whom an English farmer, feeling rightly
that leaving chance to chance was much too chancy,
hired to build an Engine of Good Fortune
in what had once been an orchard of Cox's Spiffins, causing
their genetic stock to be erased completely
when foundations were laid down for the device.

Horse-drawn wagons
brought the milled parts from Sheffield, Leeds & York, although
Le Sourd was killed by the falling spanner of a workman, leaving
his hopeful blueprints for one Hamish McPosset
to get inevitably wrong & therefore build
the grinding factory of doom we know today which
necessitated Egyptian-pyramid-style building methods until
the great flywheel, all 300 tons of it, was started up,
with a clicking of sprockets, a chattering of pulleys, re-
distributing luck, hazard & confusion on the basis
of no basis at all, so that
as the slowly accelerating thump of its mighty pistons
began to eliminate with fuzzy precision all the previously laid plans
of mice & men, Hamish McPosset himself, whilst walking
with the excessive caution one would expect of a Chance Engineer,
on a high gantry beneath the corrugated iron roof, turned
right instead of left at the end of a walkway
& fell with silent speed into the chimney which conducted smoke
from the ten coke-fuelled furnaces driving the entire operation,
& was hauled out later as the day's ashes
& buried in the last corner of the orchard remaining
in the hope that, despite the depredations of industry,
a small corner of rural England would revive,
& possibly even give rise to a new breed of Cox's Spiffin.

So it is, that these days, as we go about our business,
whether in China or the furthest tip of the South American continent,
our lives are reshuffled in a glum valley-fold of Herefordshire
by a Moloch which has not stopped since eighteen sixty seven,
although a conversion from solid to more environmentally friendly fuel
was made in nineteen seventy four, & the whole enterprise
costs you, me & the country absolutely nothing, being
a model of economics in a state of free fall whose
inexplicable self-regulation is a cause for wonder & puzzlement,
& the workers who tend its operation,
& the cheerful postcards from the absentee landlord who has leased out the
terrain,
& the countless coach parties of visitors who solemnly file past it,
& the building of new roads which lead to & from it,
& the installation of ever more complex early-warning systems –
all this is futile, as the archaic apparatus is, after all,
a self-fuelling, coke & steam propelled *perpetuum mobile*,
that is to say, it is impossible for anyone to modernise or repair it,

or invest in it, or inspect it, or even install child-proofing,
because what will happen will uselessly happen
thru an unspeakable law of mechanics that is not in the textbooks,
& to install child-proofing is to guarantee that boys on the roof
will fall thru a skylight to the concrete floor two hundred feet below, so it is
best not to hasten the inevitable by doing anything about it, & quite
                                                                    honestly
"unspeakable" is the word one has to use because people
who visit the colossus do not speak, there is a severe hush everywhere
even as the thing itself clashes & hammers,
indeed, apart from those who go expressly to see it
(& then for the remainder of their lifetimes refrain from speaking of it)
there is what one might call a conspiracy of not-talking-about it,
 so that even maps do not include the orchard's location
& neither Jacques le Sourd nor Hamish McPosset are mentioned
in Encyclopaedia Britannica or any other work of reference,
& there are no signposts along the main road out of Worcester,
although the bus drivers somehow know the way.

Yet, at home, standing in a garden in the silence of a summer night,
smelling the heavy, brackish, heart-leeching perfume
that rises from an accidentally disturbed bush of *I-Forget-the-Name*,
& looking up into the blackness across which Mavis Doolittle's comet
is making its millennial way towards the end of the universe,
& smoking, perhaps, one of your Ataturk cigarettes,
drawing gentle puffs of piratical fume deep into your poor lungs,
you will look back on your life & see how everything went wrong,
but subtly, faintly, not in any major way you could claim sympathy for,
as if you had once turned a corner too late to see the one you love
turn a corner ahead of you, so that you just went on not having seen her,
& although there is a saying: *what you can't see, can't see you either*,
this is actually a popular adage I would like to take the opportunity here
of passionately denouncing as a damned fallacy, a lie, an imposture,
because however quickly gone it may be,
the moment of not being seen is worth having, & I would like
to suggest, therefore, that you close your eyes
& imagine for yourself the infernally clanking locomotive,
& then open your eyes again, exhale gently, a microsecond closer to death,
& see the *Liebesweh*, the *Ripefrock*, the *Spot-on-the-Lung*, the *Odorendrum*
whose scent fills the night air & dims the stars & makes your heart slow
& ravishes you upon your walk around the garden
before you finally enter the house for a nightcap
of that faintly resinous Mixed Blessing you like so much
& a slice of Trembling Bulldog before bed.

KEITH JEBB

MOSQUITO

Don't imagine we chose to worship
the mosquito. It chose us. Our
blood coursing its gossamer veins

it had to feel as we did. And
without us it would die. To
take to your arm a god that gives

you the lump and itch of her
being is to be kissed by good
fortune. A baby's first bite

was its blood-bond to the tribe
a celebration held in voiceless
stinging joy. If a child

remained unbitten or its skin
refused to puff and smart
it was an outcast by its

second year, abandoned
on the smooth excrescent hill
which is the earth's bite from

the sun. So as it drank
the water from the ground
it might accept the child's

thin blood. Mosquitos fly
from the belly of the sun
as it sinks blood-red

to the mountains. At dawn
they speed off east taking
the honey of our limbs

to fuel the day. So when
one summer the bites refused
to heal, when old and young

turned yellow, sour and died
what could we think? Perhaps
our blood was tainted and

our gods would die? But still
they came at night, the sun
rose bright and warmer

though the pools they called
us to grew rank, so we almost
could not bear to say

our long bare-torsoed
evening prayers. Have
you ever seen your family

murdered by the source
of all your life? Seen love
turn evil for no reason

you can find? We lift our
arms up to the sky and
ask what we have done

but the sun just smiles.
Heat buzzes through the day.
I will not be the last

to die. I write this for
the worshippers of tree
and flower and stream

the pale and bloodless ghosts.

Anansi's Transformations

by Graeme Wright

JOHN AGARD

Weblines

Bloodaxe, £9.95
ISBN 1 85224 480 1

SUCCESSFUL POETS ARE like magicians, famous for what they do not rather than what they do show. It is the linguistic sleight-of-hand which leaves the reader asking, "how did he do that?" as the next trick begins. John Agard is just such a poet; successful – Casa de las Americas prize, Paul Hamlyn Award *et al* – and, as readers of his previous collections can testify, a specialist in word trickery.

With his latest book, *Weblines*, Agard retreads to a degree the territory of *From The Devil's Pulpit* but whereas in 1997 Lucifer was the image- and gender-changing confederate of the poetry, here he/she/it is Anansi, the smooth-tongued spider character of West African and Caribbean folklore. Part god, part mischievous spirit, Anansi adapts the world to his/her/its current metamorphosis, be it television celebrity chatting to Kilroy, trespasser in the Queen's bath or member of the landed gentry complete with top hat and eight cups of tea. Agard relates Anansi's adventures with a purity of language and sharpness of humour all too rare now in today's too serious society while his mastery of rhythm pulsates across every page. The Anansi poems which form the first third of the book can almost be sung as they are read, so strong is their music. Some ring with the simplicity of nursery rhymes while others, though not complex, require a more thorough understanding, an unraveling of the many cultural strands with which they are composed:

so I headed for England
land of hope and unfinished glory
like Schubert's symphony

leaving Amsterdam to Surinam spinners
and Paris to Martinique weavers.

('The Embodiment')

The second part of the book, 'Limbo Dancer In Dark Glasses,' is altogether more philosophically pure with its flexi-limbed protagonist, an extension of spider hero as universal limbo dancer, stretching between different continents and politics, histories and histrionics in a blur of back-bending metaphor. Agard challenges us to remember the role of limbo dancer as onboard entertainer for white slavers between Africa and America, a role which still finds a place in hotel cabarets from Mombasa to Montego Bay. The language in these poems is taut and finely balanced, finding its own music, charting its own passage between Port Elizabeth and Port of Spain, Georgetown and Greenham Common. These are poems which reverberate with the injustices of the ages, point no unjustly accusing fingers and offer no false solutions. The constant straining of the limbo dancer here becomes everyone's burden:

And when limbo dancer revealed ankles
bruised with the memory of chains
                    it meant nothing to them

So limbo dancer bent over backwards
                    & danced
                    & danced
                    & danced

until from every limb
flowed a trail of red.

('Limbo Dancer At Immigration')

'Man To Pan', the final part of the trilogy, uses steel drums as a pivotal theme from which ripples of sound, rhyme and thought spread, literally, across the page. At times the words, even individual letters, form patterns while rhythms appear and change constantly like a well-rehearsed samba band; the poetry here is charged with a freshness, a willingness to experiment with and challenge the frontiers of language. Caribbean patois jostles with West African occultism in a thunderous celebration of many musics, both man-made and natural. The swirling rhythms of carnival blend effortlessly with the pounding "bamboo tamboo" in uniting continents and sealing the web:

in that web of light
ah feel like panorama night
and ah hear meself say
oyo oyo

oyo shango
ah glad to see you man
accept this offering
of pan

On one level *Weblines* provides us with further evidence of Agard's ceaseless imagination and knowledge of folklore while on a higher level it crackles with the electricity of language and form; there can be no preconceptions with this poetry, so fresh is the imagery, so abstract the symbolism. *Weblines* demands, and warrants, attention. This book can only help to further John Agard's status as one of our most consistent, culture-crossing spokesmen.

> **Graeme Wright writes:**
> I write poetry and have had work published in three anthologies to date. I have also written articles which have been published in newspapers as well as *The Lady* magazine and short stories which have yet to see a wider audience. I am a member of the Bridgewater Hall Writers group in Manchester who have their first anthology published this month and am currently working on a cycle of poems about local railway stations.

Griefs and Wonders

By Hugh Macpherson

MICHAEL LONGLEY

The Weather in Japan
Cape, £8.00
ISBN 0 224 06043 0

Selected poems
Cape, £8.00
ISBN 0 224 05035 4

MICHAEL LONGLEY IS recognised as one of the most moving and accomplished poets of our time, and *The Weather in Japan* is a book that continues that achievement, with nearly eighty new poems. When you open the collection, you're immediately drawn in by a series of sharply-observed lyric verses, and you're well into the book before you stop to catch breath, and take more deliberate account of what is going on.

The impression is of someone who is himself, not overwhelmed, but almost battered by the multiplicity, force and beauty of what exists and takes place around us.

In 'Pale Butterwort' he begins with the realisation that "Pale butterwort's smoky blue colours your eyes ..." But only two lines later "a buzzard distracted me" and "the papery purr of the dragonflies' Love-flight..." and "with so much happening overhead I forgot the pale butterwort there on the ground". He returns to the flower and to the woman whose eyes and "every feature" he had been thinking of, but in between he's taken a path by the buzzard's "skraik or screel" – not just one account of its cry but the two versions – and the insects squirming on the leaves of the carnivorous plant.

'The Lapwing' starts unsettled because of a poisoned swan, but the other bird takes his attention and:

...\"Why me?"
The lapwing replies and falters like a bi-plane
Above her nest. "Why me?" The lapwing and I
watch over each other and we speak in tongues.

In eight lines here we get the fine nuanced observation of what's around us but also a lurking sense of menace – of another side to things for us and for lapwings – and the shade of mystery that goes along with this, the need to "watch over each other" and the speaking in tongues that indicates some shared understanding – but of what, exactly, we can't say. In 'The Comber' there is a brief sighting of an otter in the short moment that a wave is turning itself into a breaker – an encounter that prevents the animal getting the human "scent in her nostril", but it's a meeting that's normally impossible because of "the uproar of my presence. My unforgivable shadow in the sand ..." The terms of existence don't readily allow such moments.

As the collection unfolds it's clear that, as in all Longley's previous work, this fine evocation of birds and beasts and flowers implies no neglect of what human life is up to. They are a part of our experience of the world that is set against the darker moments that affect us and the beasts too. Already in these poems such moments are hovering at the edge of things: even if they are kept out of the celebratory instant, they may reappear. It's the balance between celebration and harm or menace, and the mystery of just how that balance is established –

certainly not by our control and decision – that give the power and resonance to Longley's poems. He's found a way of setting out the best and the worst together, and leaving them not in contradiction but in some intimation of their true relationship to each other – apprehended but not quite understood, felt but not seen or able to be dealt with by a purely rational view: all the more forceful for that.

Seamus Heaney's comment that Longley is "a custodian of griefs and wonders" is exact. "Custodian" expresses precisely the concern and the care of the presentation, and the contrast of content is part of the real matter of what we receive here. Sometimes that balance and contrast are brought together and made explicit, as in 'The Yellow Teapot' where a betrayal in the first verse produces both a curse and "a quilt of quilt names to keep you warm in the dark". Accordingly, the second verse offers an equal number of lines of evocation in order to – well, it's not clear if it's to counteract or console – but in any event to offer something from the positive side of life as counterbalance, as resistance, to what went before.

When he deals with human suffering and the world of nature together, it's not a diminution of the human hurt, but an expansion of it, something that the rest of creation feels with us. So, in 'A Poppy', considering an image in Homer where the doomed soldier's helmet is already –

> Lolling to one side like a poppy in a garden
> Weighed down by its seed capsule and rainwater

– the image ends by producing four hundred flower-heads, "two thousand petals overlapping... to make a cape... for a soldier's soul".

Similarly 'The Horses' begins with a tribute to horses killed on the battlefield and then, without losing sight of that, brings us to the grief of Homeric horses mourning for Patroclus.

That contrast of "griefs and wonders" gives a further resonance to the sense of history. The view back through generations shows us others struggling to balance similar experiences, and so the references to historical events, and to classical poetry, seem not extraneous but a natural adjunct to the subject matter. Even a moment of repose, "Leaning back like a lover against this beech tree's... pewter trunk", takes on extra weight from the thought of "Everybody who has teetered where these huge roots spread" and of Virgil and the landscapes of his *Eclogues* and *Georgics*.

The *Selected Poems* is Longley' s own choice from thirty years' of work. It contains a long parade of excellent poems, including about half of those from his previous book *The Ghost Orchid* – though you'd do well to get hold of that and have all of them. It's worth saying that all these books are finely produced by Cape, with well-designed covers that show a lion by Hokusai for *The Weather in Japan*, an engraving of a snipe by Jeffrey Morgan for the *Selected*, and a suitably pale bloom for *The Ghost Orchid*.

The *Selected Poems* contains some longer early poems, with elaborate rhyme-schemes and a love of paradox, in a style that recalls Marvell and Donne – poems such as 'Epithalamion', 'A Personal Statement' and 'The Hebrides'. In these and other poems from the 'sixties, it's fascinating to see how Longley deals with themes that continue to concern him in different forms at later stages. But there's no question of him producing repetitive work. Most poets who create poems of this quality have moments of writing things that seem overly-familiar to the reader. That is not a feeling you receive at any moment in these books. In 'Pascoli's Portrait' Longley observes that "a poem's little more than a wing and a prayer". Another reason for optimism on the basis of these books, therefore, for it's astonishing to see with how many poems he has made it through, on that apparently slender basis, over the years. In 'Fragment' he says:

> Forty years I've been at it, working hard,
> A poetic pro, no longer the neophyte
> I'm standing near the metalworker's yard
> And can't find the words for this starry night.

But he has, of course, in the words of his disclaimer.

Slanted and Enchanted

By Stephen Troussé

DAVID BERMAN

Actual Air

Open City Books, $12.95
ISBN 1 890447 04 8

IF YOU'VE EVER eased your way into a hungover Saturday morning with an FM radio station and had a line from some alt.country reverie snag in your head and hang around all day ... or set your alarm clock for the hour you were born, so that "every morning is an historical re-enactment" ... or wondered what would happen if the modern American smartness of Steven Wright, Stephen Malkmus and Stephin Merritt manifested itself in contemporary poetry ... then this first collection by David Berman is probably worthy of your immediate attention.

Berman first blipped on the cultural radar in the mid-nineties when he and some co-conspirators from the American rock band Pavement assembled as the Silver Jews and recorded an album of willfully eccentric shaggy dog stories. In the slack fashion of the day, the band sounded like they had just stumbled out of bed, drifting in and out of time, with a vocal holding often only a very notional relationship with tunefulness. There were some interesting lines ("What if you had to pay a nickel each time you woke up – I'd pay all the way to the poorhouse"), but, like most people, I filed it away under "interesting curiosity".

So when I came across this collection on the meagre bookshelves of a basement record shop, my expectations were slight. The precedents for rock musicians writing poetry, let's face it, are not encouraging. If Bob Dylan, Lou Reed, and – hey! – even Robbie Williams couldn't manage to write a convincing stanza or two, what chance does this guy have? At most he promised to be a kind of dazed and confused Richard Brautigan for the twenty-first century ... just what we need, right?

However, Berman has received some interesting acclaim: the book comes trailing clouds of critical glory, and beneath a back cover picture of the author, looking like someone who might have played vibes during the Big Pink sessions, Billy Collins and James Tate try to out-do each other in praising Berman to the stars. Indeed, Collins is moved so far as to exclaim "when I first read him, I thought: so this is the voice I have been waiting so long to hear, a voice, I wish in some poems, were my own". The twin poles of Tate's just-so surrealism and Collins' mundane mysticism are probably the best reference points for poetry readers coming fresh to Berman's world. A poem such as 'Classic Water' begins as an edgy elegy for an ex-girlfriend, full of more-or-less moving *Wonder Years*-style teen nostalgia, remembering how "at volleyball games her parents sat in the bleachers / like ambassadors from Indiana in all their midwestern schmaltz". But then the next lines spin off to a life less ordinary: "She was destroyed when they were busted for operating / a private judicial system within U.S. borders". Those lines might put you in mind of Oedipa Maas, stumbling across a private postal system in sixties California in Thomas Pynchon's *The Crying of Lot 49*, discovering a "secret richness and concealed density of dream". The metafictional play and fabulation of Pynchon, Barthelme, Gass and Ashbery – that American High Postmodernism – is another feature of Berman's style. And not just Berman – it's a current in many of the more interesting younger American writers, from David Foster Wallace to Dave Eggers and *McSweeney's* magazine (indeed one of Berman's poems, mentioning a man who "paints radio storms / in the basement beside a globe of Mars", sparked a long Flann O'Brien-esque letters-page debate in that magazine on where exactly one could procure such a globe).

Like Tate says, there is much to savour on each page of *Actual Air*: a character mistakenly takes the thermostat "for a dial / with which to focus the windows", a house "held nude parties fueled by five dollar bills / pulled out of birthday cards by the host, / a postal clerk with a sharp eye for grandmotherly script"; another character remembers "confessing our devotion to resemblances / on the yellowed breakdance charts / that we studied by candlelight, / like toys caught reading // their own directions". These skewed details and tangential situations are the most immediately obvious characteristic of Berman's poetry – he has a kind of genius for the off-centre insight. 'The Night Nurse Essays' begins:

... the idea was to patch together a book

that described itself over and over again,
comprised of thousands of black chains
that were dragged through green rocks and river
stairs
to arrive haunted, unscheduled and lit from above.

At its worst, *Actual Air* can seem similarly "patched together", consisting of poems that meander lazily, accumulating disconnected incidents from a notebook of quirkiness. One poem states "my statistics show that several thousand years of rain / have done little damage to the planet, / yet imagine if that amount had fallen indoors" – and it's this goofy inconsequence which can sometimes seem Berman's nervous tic, as though he feels every line should wear a party hat. The comedian Steven Wright – who once said that the first time he read a dictionary he thought it was a poem about everything – can leave you with a similar feeling after a performance of his screwball-zen one-liners – in a state of admiring but unmoved exhaustion.

There's more to Berman than cleverness, however. If there's irony, it's an irony undercut, or augmented, by a tremendous melancholy. As Justin Quinn pointed out in the last issue (p.52), when the British do irony, it's usually in the service of bathos. A recent – very funny – Paul Farley poem imagines a modern Joseph Beuys being healed not with butter and felt, but with Stork SB and I Can't Believe It's Not Butter. When Berman refers to the detritus of the modern world and mediated existence, he strikes a more plangent minor chord: a drowning man is

Pulled down through the cool green chambers,
we like to imagine him struggling awake
and suddenly realizing
he was seeing rain
in its original uncut form.

Just because we see things in inverted commas, they don't lose their capacity to astonish. In recent years this kind of balancing act between irony and melancholy has been pulled off most notably by Mark Halliday, of whom Berman is sometimes strongly reminiscent, from the suburban reveries of 'The Charm of 5.30' to the wackier musings of 'Community College in the Rain'. But it's worth bearing in mind that it took Halliday three volumes to arrive at his current pre-eminence, a distance Berman seems to have covered in this debut collection. One of the many misbegotten characters lost in Berman's poems worries that his book is "ineffective / like [...] a statue of the fastest man alive". *Actual Air* may be no more effective, but Berman is coming along in leaps and bounds. You should catch him while you can.

Of Tact and Telajune

by Gillian Allnutt

SUJATA BHATT

Augatora

Carcanet £8.95
ISBN 1 85754 381 5

CAROLE SATYAMURTI

Love and Variations

Bloodaxe £7.95
ISBN 1 85224 526 3

MIMI KHALVATI

Selected Poems

Carcanet £6.95
ISBN 1 85754 472 2

SUJATA BHATT'S FOURTH collection is a PBS Recommendation. A long poem towards the close of the book tolerantly declares:

The multicultural poem does not expect
the reader to "understand" anything.
After all, it is used to being misunderstood.

('The Multicultural Poem')

As I copy these lines, I suddenly hear "England expects ..." echoing away on the spot and wonder whether it was put there on purpose or just got in by itself.

No one is better qualified than Bhatt for the post of multicultural poet, and her ongoing preoccupation with language is much in evidence in this new collection. "What happened when the Gujarati / and the Marathi and the Hindi / I spoke / made room for the English words?" she asks in 'New

Orleans Revisited'. And in 'History is a Broken Narrative' she continues: "In an English convent school in Poona, / years later, the very very old Miss Ghaswalla / managed to change / my New Orleans style". And now she lives in Bremen. "Augatora" (eye-gate, window) is Old High German and there's Plattdeutsch here and Danish and who knows what... Of the multicultural poem she writes: "It likes the word *terracotta*".

I want to pick up on "understand". As a reader, and especially as a reviewer, I'm intolerant of poetry I cannot understand, intolerant of my own ignorance or stupidity. But I never mind not fully understanding a poem of Sujata Bhatt's and I think it's because I don't feel mocked by it. I believe it will sit and smile and wait until I am able to grasp the depth of its simplicity. It's not that I haven't read enough books, rather that I haven't yet lived enough lives.

There's a tact in this work that manifests itself in different ways. It comes as empathy in 'A Swimmer in New England Speaks': a girl with a "shrivelled polio leg" is falling in love over three pages and a terrible hope is in me as I read. And in 'Green Amber in Riga' I am as amazed as the poem's dedicatee, Gunnar Cirulis, to whom the Red Army has suddenly returned his family house:

"This was our home – this was
our home ..." you kept on
repeating with such joy –
your feet emphatic on the floor.

Of course I know that that "emphatic" is doing its linguistic footwork – but the fact remains that, however closely I analyse the technique of this poem, there's something else between the lines I can't pin down that lets me share its wonder.

Tact works differently in 'Voice of the Unwanted Girl', where the lines are spoken by an aborted female foetus –

Look, mother,
look for the place where you have sent me.
Look for the unspeakable,
for the place that can never be described.

– and in 'The Hole in the Wind', a long poem written for radio about the island of Juist and all its shipwrecks, where the poet addresses the ghosts of the drowned –

Speak to me and I will listen
even as you utter all that is unspeakable.

"Unspeakable" seems to mean both "incapable of being put into words" and "horrifying". The horror suffuses both poems and yet there is nothing in-your-face violent or disgusting about the imagery in either. By leaving it unspoken, the unspeakable becomes more so.

There is an overall coherence to this collection. The first lines of the title poem –

Windoge, vindauga, wind eye –
the hole, the opening, the opening out
into the wind, the hole.
The wind blowing into the house.

– in echoing those of 'The Hole in the Wind', open the world of the one to the other and each poem gains immeasurably.

Carole Satyamurti

Love and Variations is Carole Satyamurti's fourth collection. There's a diligence here, a suspending of disbelief, a sincere attempt to imagine how any of us, had we lived in Chantérac during the last war, might have come to betray to the local Gauleiter the "single, peaceable Jew", Jacques Demartin:

Did someone with a gun at their throat, and a son in
the Maquis, seize
a wisp of hope – as one might try to soft-soap an
ordinary bully,
as *I'll take you to where there are otters,* or something
else rare and harmless?
('The Jew of Chantérac')

And in case you'd still like to think yourself capable of the grand gesture, turn to 'Les Autres *or* Mr Bleaney's Other Room' and be prepared to join in that hotel bedroom the "sad company who've seen / themselves summed up by chintz and candlewick .... and realise / how you have buttressed your identity / with fragile props, convinced yourself of your / uniqueness". Being old (or whatever it is one is after 50) is a rueful, honest business.

"Love has struck me as a painful fact / I didn't know I knew" writes Carole Satyamurti towards the end of the twelve-poem sequence about her brother's death at the age of 50. 'Boy with a Fish' cannot have been easy to write. She "treads with the delicacy of a tight-rope walker": balancing a bare biography (expensive schooling, brief failed marriage, office job, benders, bland diary entries) with a lightly proffered "analysis" (an exacting father, a mother's "early luke-warm welcome" , "a skin too few", the loss of that "non-renewable resource of confidence"). The sequence, the way it works (and it does), appears to be related to Satyamurti's work at the Tavistock Clinic where, she writes, her main interest is in "relating psycho-analytic ideas to the stories people tell about them-selves". She balances, too, the sordid details of her brother's once-hidden daily life – "All furniture / engulfed by takeaways, / thousands of crushed tissues, / ruined clothes" – with this in the poem's final lines –

> In death, you became
> more than material – pharoah, famine victim,
> soldier, the dead, grey Christ. Every human.

In the book's opening section, all the poems are addressed to "you", a fastidious you but one suscep-tible to the humour that is part of love in later life –

> Your flawless eye is bound to see
> the dross of accumulation like a thickening
> around the waist. That's age for you.

> ('I'll Show You My House')

These are civilised poems, penned with a light playful touch that still leaves room for the less than plain sailing of love. The other's need for solitude is hard to bear; and yet it is the poems that deal with absence that please me the most:

> know that I'll receive silence from you
> as though it were a letter, and be glad, seeing
> there can always be letters, while even small
> stacks of days like clean canvases are precious, few.

> ('On Not Writing a Letter from Iona')

Mimi Khalvati

Like Satyamurti, Mimi Khalvati began publishing comparatively late in life. As if long-dammed indeed, the words pour out. Whereas the poems from *In White Ink* (1991) are self-contained and short(ish), and selections from *Mirrorwork* (1995) mix self-contained poems with extracts from three sequences, those from *Entries on Light* (1997), comprising more than half of this *Selected*, don't

stop for titles but have to be listed by first lines and separated from each other by an asterisk. Yet it's almost as if, with these last, the poet has gone full circle and come back to self-containment, as if the poems were pieces in mosaic or mirrorwork.

The 'Entries' vary greatly in form. The one beginning "First you invite me ..." lets its words tumble out over each other in Khalvati's response to the photograph she's received from her friend of themselves at tea in the garden:

> And the apple tree just visible
> where bright light grows on a shrub I'd know, if it
> weren't
> for those clumps of flowering light you knew
> I'd like
> has no flowers.

There is a sense of rush, but also a studied delight in complicated syntax. With Khalvati I find myself compulsively checking out lines like the above to make sure they work – and I often fail. It's as if these poems are a musical score rather than a recording: each reading means putting the poem together, reassembling the lines as you go. I admire them very much and regret my laziness.

Though she grew up on the Isle of Wight, Khalvati was born in Tehran. Sometimes, as in 'An Iranian professor I know...', she is concerned, like Sujata Bhatt, with the impossibility of translating from one language to another:

> ...no one has come up with
> the English for *Saheb-del*. Is it a name
> for the very thing that won't translate?

In 'Rubaiyat', a poem from her first volume, she records her closeness to and distance from her grandmother, Telajune:

> I have inherited her tools: her anvil,
> her axe, her old scrolled mat, but not her skill;
> and who would choose to chip at sugar-blocks
> when sugar-cubes are boxed beside the till?

And in 'Prayer', from her second volume, she again signals her unique multicultural mix of ancient and modern, philosophical and practical, Persian and British: "Prayer is a time of day / that on a winding stair / greets itself" and "Prayer / is like watering the plants, / popping out to get the paper, / a trundling, pottering".

ALISON CROGGON
ELEGY

Weeping cannot be said: intolerable
overswelling, fist without edges,
a hand dreamt beneath water, a mouth
turned down as if it could speak, as if tears
were not what we're made of –

the rain breaking through boughs
its cloudy body, bending dumb grass
under its dewlings, what does it know,
innocent water, swelling the cellulose
membranes, lubricating the bladed mouths
of beetles and ants, all-dimensional
medium of tinily panting cells,
blue breast of the world, our nakedness –
what does it know. Imagine
each molecule scarred by its incarnations, how
infinite sorrow could be – but here, clapped
into air, incandescent droplets, no
curse of consciousness hurts it. So are we
mostly, this lovely matter, drummed
on the tingling skin of sense to this
minute being, which clasps and encloses,
lamped by this motion to self. So small,
but everything there is! Hugging our wounds
we are most human – delight blazes us
to godliness, sheer as broken water,
griefless and borderless, wanting nothing.

If we were but that. The voice
across the twilit grass, calling me home,
inhabits me always, although I scorch
it out of my mind. What hurts most
is remembered beauty, a lost hand stroking
a brush through infant hair, the smell
of mouth in a breathing room. And you,
hand I will never touch, why does your death
prick this skin? All weeping running together
into a single grief, me, huddled small
against infinite flanks. One warmth pressed
on emptiness fades, and all warmth dims,

returning its grief to the brighter moment
where my heavier pulse forces the now
to impure brilliance, neither godly
nor godless, humbled in history, human.

K. M. DERSLEY
THE TERRITORIES OF BUDGER NOTTCUTT

And shall it come to pass they'll
put roads over the allotments and chicken runs
of our forefathers?
And car parks "adorn" where once Budger Nottcutt
reigned supreme as hard case?
It may be so, for has not W.H. Smith moved
from one side of the road to the other?

Hasn't Owen Owen inherited with an
almighty sprawl of goods that very
place where we sat of nights in the caff
while teenaged Iranian sailors about to
be sent home queued up to slobber over
60-year-old "Auntie"?
(Weren't they glad to get hold of an Englishwoman
of whatever vintage?)

To deplore change, cunningly
accepting it in so doing
was always the task of a bard,
and to celebrate *the hell of it*.

Do not even now massive "piles"
erected by Dutch architects
hang over the Orwell and obliterate
the pathway where we heard Tony Cousins shriek
with the old mocking Gainsborough Estate shrillness
in Woody Woodpecker mode
before unerotically and outrageously
dropping his sinkwhite briefs?

RITA ANN HIGGINS
THEY ALWAYS GET CURRIED CHIPS

Between her supermarket sing song
and the endless gossip she loves
Dolly's voice is nearly gone.

What scandal the builders throw her
is piffle, compared to when
the sisters-in-law come round.

Every extension is taken apart
brick by adulterous brick
they know the foot fall
and back to front baseball cap

of every builder who's doing it
with the wife's sister
or that skinny man with the hippy hair
they know him down to the birth mark
on his lovely arse.

They see the cracks in every
brick and mortar give-and-take
that was hammered out in back seats
below in condom alley valley,

where the hoods sell ecstasy
and good for nothing cars
with nare a number plate
not to mind a log book.

The extension is the thing
they call it the granny flat
it takes the harm out of it,
like, one owner, mint condition
woman driver kind of shite.

It's not just small talk, it's all talk
instead of good morning
it's good extension
happy May day has become
happy granny flat day.

"She has three and a half kids and a lean-to"
(god bless the mark)
"my rafters' going up a Friday"
"my plumber is nearly upon me"
"my roofer is roofing like billio"

Where will the big dogs go now
that's what I'd like to know
at the end of our row
there's one as big as a horse.

They keep him
and his four sets of teeth
in a back yard
full of broken busses and road signs,
the new extension will cover him
an overcoat of concrete,
molar drive.

Dolly's new extension
will take your eye out
it will have every doodad.
A couch that won't burn
no matter what
buttons that bring on the foot stools,

a picture of a boy in blue
with a tear on his cheek
a remote control
that dominates the curtains
a dining room table
that goes inside itself
a grandfather clock that belts out rave
and Spanish sign language

The extension means more than space,
her status will rise in the estate
so it was written on the bingo book.

The extension will tower above the hedge
the neighbours fashioned
to stop seeing Dolly
smoke a chunk of the midweek.

As for the two up and two downers
she pities them, she'd tell you herself.
I pity them poor bastards
with nothing to show for themselves
only two ups and two downs.

Look at me, I could keep lodgers
I could keep a small village in that granny flat
and still have room to spare
when the sisters-in-law come round.

And come round they do and often
they talk back-to-front baseball caps
they talk shape, they talk size
when it comes to it
size is everything
they talk back seat gobbledegook
nothing is really sacred,

mind you they don't do politics or piss artists
but they do do priests, and how.
Tired of talking, it's time for food,

they always get curried chips
they rarely get planning permission.

BOB KAVEN

THE NEXT TIME WE MEET

The next time we meet, I will hand you this poem.
The temperature will hover a little above 60.
Burning like Cuban leaf, the air will hold
In today's stained fingers, the irreproducible

Scent of London. The color of the clouds
Will be that of a good English gouache, a color
Like tea. Somebody tautly Conservative,
            virtually puckered,
Will complain in the House of Commons

That now these same clouds are colored European.
If the two of us were drinking scrumpy cider
Out of pint glasses in front of the Museum Tavern – ;
If the two of us were standing on a damp night

Before the British Museum on Great Russell Street,
And our ears, enhanced with the subtle
        electronics of imagination,
Were actually tuned to the ancient frequencies,
We would definitely hear the granite

Dignity of the Assyrian Collection assiduously
Cleansing the floors, polishing history into the corridors
Like paste wax. After a clamshell-colored English winter,
        I will hand you this poem.
I'll meet you here, at the back of Pied Bull Yard,

Perhaps in late April, as the weather's clearing,
In the wine bar downstairs. I'll be late, of course –
        I'm always late –;
And you'll have kept yourself busy, drawing
Rings with your glass in the condensation on the table,
And nibbling at a plate of stilton and crackers.
The manager's nice. She'll treat you right
While you wait. We'll get up from the table;
We'll cross the street, and dissolve ourselves
        in history,

The universal solvent. We will be blinded
By the utter thingyness of the artifacts of this world
And their shoddy glamor. Nor will we see
        the endless queue
Of the Empire of the Dead, keeping pace with us

Along these corridors, abrading everything like entropy;
Inhaling the vapors of our breath like food.

Seduction with Conversation

By David Wheatley

WILLIAM EMPSON

Complete Poems

Edited by John Haffenden
Allen Lane, £30
ISBN 0 71 399 87 5

I'VE ALWAYS BEEN interested in William Empson, but moving to Hull this year I'd no idea of the sort of connection with him that I was about to acquire: buying a house, I discovered that the vendor was his son and that the tiles on the fireplace had come from the great man's Hampstead study. As if one Empsonian living-room ornament wasn't enough, I then got my hands on the enormously lavish new *Complete Poems*. The cover painting is David Hockney's *Great Pyramid at Giza with Broken Head from Thebes*, and a Tutankhamen's hoard of Empsoniana it turned out to be.

For those used to the long out-of-print Hogarth Press *Collected* the size of this edition will come as a surprise: this is a big book, a very big book. If the notes are longer than the poems, which have you got, a prose or verse book? This was Empson's question to a publisher in 1930. What would he say to John Haffenden's efforts as an editor, yielding almost four hundred pages of prose to his 110 of verse? Judging by his various comments on the subject (poems without notes are like "a seduction without conversation") he'd be delighted. Still, the sheer amount of editorial foreplay is startling. Empson's choice of an extract from Buddha's Fire Sermon as an epigraph elicits thirteen pages of comment; thumbing backwards and forwards between svelte poem and bulky notes is like nothing so much as watching Dr Johnson chat up Kate Moss, to mix up the poet's seduction metaphor.

Crossing the road with Empson once, T. S. Eliot announced that the most important thing for a poet was "to write as little as possible". It's advice the younger poet took unfortunately to heart. *Poems* appeared in 1935 and *The Gathering Storm* in 1940, and then ... nothing, or almost nothing. The number of previously unpublished poems here is negligible, none of them from after the occasional piece 'The Birth of Steel' written for a royal visit to Sheffield in 1954; a long Joycean poem "telling people what to do in bed" has been withheld by the executors. Far from being regretful about it, Empson was even defiant about his post-war silence: "I am inclined to congratulate myself on stopping writing", he told Christopher Ricks in 1975.

Yet, for a few early years, Empson had looked unstoppable. An appearance in *Cambridge Poetry 1929* brought him to the attention of F. R. Leavis, who praised him in *New Bearings in English Poetry* and read him to Wittgenstein, before the inevitable falling-out (Empson was never disciple material, unlike Leavis's other tip for the future, the unfortunate Ronald Bottrall). Also in 1929, Empson was deprived of a Cambridge fellowship when contraceptives were found in his room, a fiasco commemorated in 'Warning to undergraduates'. The following year the young reprobate wiped Magdalen's eye by publishing the brilliant *Seven Types of Ambiguity*, helping to create an audience for exactly the sort of poetry he was writing: neo-metaphysical lyrics of a dazzling complexity and wit like nothing else in modern poetry, least of all the "geared-up propaganda boys in Oxford" he affectionately parodies in 'Just a Smack at Auden'. Here are the opening two stanzas of the 1928 poem 'To an Old Lady':

> Ripeness is all; her in her cooling planet
> Revere; do not presume to think her wasted.
> Project her no projectile, plan nor man it;
> Gods cool in turn, by the sun long outlasted.
>
> Our earth alone given no name of god
> Gives, too, no hold for such a leap to aid her;
> Landing, you break some palace and seem odd;
> Bees sting their need, the keeper's queen invader.

The "Old Lady" is Empson's mother, addressed as a foreign planet from the earth, whose lack of a god's name "is compared to some body of people [...] without fundamental beliefs as a basis for action" (Empson's note). The projectiles point to the poet's interest in space-travel (which would later produce the memorably titled essay 'Donne the Spaceman'); even if he tries to land on her planet, he may only do more harm than good. Empson's ferocious anti-Christianity seems to have complicated his relationship with his mother, whose "planet" he says is visible only in darkness, a line he came to see as foretelling how good his mother would be to him during his Fellowship crisis the following year.

Emotional awkwardness, typically suffocated or suffocatingly strong feeling, would remain a prime Empson theme. Examples include the great 'Missing Dates' ("Slowly the poison the whole bloodstream fills") and 'Villanelle' ("It is the pain, it is the pain endures"), poems that achieved almost holy writ status among Empson's Movement imitators. The interaction of the sexes is described with an entomologist's curiosity, as in 'Arachne', whose "disastrously proud" queen spider kills her mate. Examples of successful coupledom are rarer, and tend to be shortlived. For once the earth really does move for the lovers in 'Aubade', set during a Japanese earthquake, but what lingers in the mind is the fidgety leave-taking that follows, and the hints of inner turbulence behind those thrusting short sentences (compare MacNeice's 'House on a Cliff'):

Hours before dawn we were woken by the quake.
My house was on a cliff. The thing could take
Bookloads off shelves, break bottles in a row.
Then the long pause and then the bigger shake.
It seemed the best thing to be up and go.

And far too large for my feet to step by.
I hoped that various buildings were brought low.
The heart of standing is you cannot fly.

The notes offer one of the many tantalizing foretastes of what we can expect from Haffenden's biography: moving to England, Empson's Japanese lover worked as a nanny to the young David Wevill, whose father called the police when an over-enthusiastic Empson turned up drunk.

These poems, the anthology pieces, will be familiar enough to most readers, but what of his other work? Some of the juvenilia, like 'Two Centos', have a wistful inkhorn charm at best, little scholarly *jeux d'esprit*. As they suggest, Empson had a wicked ear for parody, not just of Auden & co., but the

"stupefyingly reiterative" Gertrude Stein ('Poem about a Ball in the Nineteenth Century') and, more in homage than in parody, Marvell in 'Flighting for Duck', a fine sketch of the alluvial Yorkshire marsh land where he grew up. Another tribute poem, 'Homage to the British Museum', takes the dryness of scholarship as its theme but fairly crackles rather than creaks with phrase-making: "There is a Supreme God in the ethnological section", "People are continually asking one the way out", and in conclusion, "Let us offer our pinch of dust all to this God, / And grant his reign over the entire building".

Then there are the difficult poems, like 'High Dive' and 'Letter IV'; densest of all is 'Bacchus', whose alcoholic theme may explain the hangover-like effects induced by trying to puzzle it out. The political poems of *The Gathering Storm* mark a notable shift towards a more limpid style, as in 'Courage Means Running', 'The Beautiful Train', 'China' and the long 'Autumn on Nan-Yüeh', written "under refugee conditions" after the Japanese invasion of Manchuria. It was during this period, deprived of his books, that Empson apparently typed out the whole of *Othello* from memory for his students. In the same spirit 'Autumn on Nan-Yüeh' concentrates on getting on with the job, in spite of doubts and distractions:

Politics are what verse should
Not fly from, or it goes all wrong.
I feel the force of that all right,
And had I speeches they were song.
But really, does it do much good
To put in verse however strong
The welter of a doubt at night
At home, in which I too belong?

But then, all of a sudden, the welter of doubt got too strong and the poetry stopped. One of his final poems was 'Let it Go', a resonant six-liner from the war about stopping writing:

It is this blankness is the real thing strange.
The more things happen to you the more you can't
Tell or remember even what they were.

The contradictions cover such a range.
The talk would talk and go so far aslant.
You don't want madhouse and the whole thing
there.

Empson didn't mind his poets being mad, but seems to have made a conscious decision not to join their company if that was the price of keeping going. Instead what we got were *Milton's God, The Structure of Complex Words* and *Using Biography*. As prose books, I wouldn't want to be without them, though reading his essays on the Faust legend I can't help wondering whether his poetic Mephistopheles ever came visiting, asking him to reconsider. Compared to madness, lucidity isn't really such a bad deal though; and as poetic lucidities go, Empson's is exemplary.

Memories Regained

by Greg Partridge

CRAIG RAINE

A la Recherche du Temps Perdu

Picador £8.00
ISBN 0 330 37576 8

CRAIG RAINE'S LATEST book comprises a single elegy, but one that encompasses the subjects which that venerable term "elegy" has long and variously defined as matter for a special kind of poetry: the transience of things of this world, of mind's reflection, of mourning. But if one is to define an elegy by its subject matter rather than its tone, then the success of the poem is perhaps elemental to its acceding to such a definition, as much as that definition is elemental to the ambition or purpose that the tone betrays.

If Raine's ambition feels rather variable in this work, it could be that his acceptance of the responsibility to elegize, and his construction of a narrative in which memories are revivified and deliberated, constitute the whole of the poem. It begins with a powerful recreation of mood and setting – the cremation of his former lover:

> *Doleo*, I am in pain, I grieve.
> And everyone thinks I am being brave.
>
> *Ignis, ignis*, masculine, fire:
> at St. Pancras Crematorium, I stare,
>
> light-headed with caffeine,
> at the light-oak coffin,
>
> wondering what I feel, where I stand.
> *Vulnus, vulneris*, neuter, a wound.

And, beautifully, we change key to learn about the lost person, those minor things that have just been removed from the world; small details that become the elegizer's preserve:

> "That – and no more, and it is everything."
> Details that make you cringe
>
> will make the reader see,
> see the self you showed to me.

Amazingly, most of the rest of the poem consists of these "details", ordered into a complex pattern of recorded happenstance and remembered events, intended to make a verbal memorial that only the poet could have created – a never less than instructive challenge that the poet has set for himself.

Of course an elegy might move us regardless of its accuracy of detail, but accurate details obviously aren't going to persuade us of the poet's powers to elegize. Raine's willingness to display these details offers a sense of earnest persuasion but also patience. His elegy is preoccupation more than resolute recall of things past:

> I sentimentalize
> and then revise.
>
> *Iter, itineris*, neuter, a journey.
> Without end. Where the road is empty.

Still, it is detail that emerges. Whatever his ability to get us to feel her former existence, we aren't meant to envy her for this memorial any more than we would envy her experience of him.

Is she, could she be, complicit in his present poetic design? This was not a relationship of thorough-going happiness, for either person, but we learn of rather a lot that she could only have endured, from his dirty letters, his preoccupation with her unwanted body hair, even his threatened fickleness contingent upon sexual favors.

Ah, the poor girl, we shall indeed lament, and not because she is deceased. Intimate settings and personal failings are presented as if divorced from the person from whom they obtain. Even the reconstructed scenes in which both parties appear in unflattering, if hardly peculiar, exertion, are not always depicted in a memorable way, and the poet appears as harried in remembrance as he does when the two were fighting.

Better is the immitigable purport, that of incineration of the beloved's body, shown to tempt the poet into remembrance, as the transformative nature of temptation itself harries him in a familiar uncurling form:

I watch the coffin vanish
to Mozart on tape, its varnish

about to come up in blisters
and burst into a boa

of full-length, rustling fire

Temptation is also thwarted:

I'd stub a fag out on the floor
And say, *Beautiful. Just leave it there.*

And it is refuted:

When I left, you went through my letters,
Burning out filth with your cigarette.

With memories so baldly reproduced, the poet's memory gives the impression of being somewhat unkempt no matter how selective of detail. Much of the detail here possesses proper names, and the more familiar the personage the more hokey the related events tend to sound (Sylvia Plath's name even comes up, with respect to the deceased's own poetry). The living literati stuff that might fall within public purview, if the public cared, feels more like a playback for our benefit, than any sort of evocation of character. AIDS, still a disease more often associated with proper names than demography, has a far more implacable presence, as if imminent in the act of elegizing:

The AIDS I guessed

and didn't guess.
Was your request a request?

Or a threat? Or a subtle plea?
I guess I didn't want to see.

Even in this poem alive with real-time remembrance, AIDS is obliquely alluded to:

You're everywhere. So it isn't odd
if there are traces of you in my blood.

More than any ruefully collected keepsake, the threat of AIDS takes dominion in the elegy itself.

I think the work of memory in the instance of this affair comes across as unrewarding in troubling respects. Neither the off-kilter, skipping and slogging meter, nor the often inventive and amusing off-rhymes serve to create memorial verse memorable in itself; only a poet might be able to recollect in verse, but Raine doesn't transmit any such experience.

Throughout much of *A la Recherche du Temps Perdu* there seems to be a superimposition of non-metrical verse upon couplets hardly more substantial than their typographical depiction. Raine's narrative rhythm does not invoke some hypothetical uniform beat, either temporal or measured regularity, upon which to hear his memories remade. Rather I hear an imaginary, unmetered plain speech that needn't be recollected to contrast the flow of Raine's lines into broader cadences of sense around his little couplets.

It is a metrically cunning performance, sufficient in flexibility to be funny, rueful, and quietly aghast without ever submitting to any uncomfortable couplet rules.

But given the almost bullying accountancy of his memories, the routinely assertive lists of facts and thwarted fancies alike, it would be poor sportsmanship not to admit that certain portions are just plain indifferent verse, narrative recitation at its worst: a list of doings.

There is a good deal of recollection, of the "You did your this, and then you did your that" sort. The poet recalls musicians humming over music, memories that overlap, where intimacy and familiarity become one – "we were on top of each other". I wish Raine had tried, and perhaps even Proust only *tried*, to describe the nature of memories not yet conscious, so that they may somehow arrive "there". Instead Raine orders his vignettes and quotations into a composition that amplifies the distance from those reconstructions and restagings, so that emotional ingress of memory may be wittily depicted –

I was having the chocolate sponge,
you were having a cold revenge

– but Raine always seems to be able to do this sort of thing well. It is the not the texture of memory so much as the textures of those things that would trigger it, and Raine demonstrates that wonderfully. But I'm not sure the poet has risked quite so much as he ultimately suggests:

You difficult, lovely, lost masterpiece,
this is my purpose.

To make you real.

Fait accompli? I don't think so, but there is much *I* won't forget, either.

Greg Partridge writes:
I'm not a poet, just a newspaper reporter, which sort of isn't writing at all. I post on Amazon very occasionally because so much of what is found there, and even in "real" reviews, is merrily oblivious to any other reader's personal forbearance of bad writing, because poetry enhances life first and most essentially by not being anything else. Other than that, the only thing worth knowing about me is that I am very interested in education, both that of primary school students as well as older kids. I'm 29 years old and live in Atascadero, a vintner's haven on the central coast of California.

Saving the Best

by Jane Holland

COLETTE BRYCE

The Heel of Bernadette

Picador £6.99
ISBN 0 330 37193 2

POLLY CLARK

Kiss

Bloodaxe £6.95
ISBN 1 85224 535 2

AMANDA DALTON

How To Disappear

Bloodaxe £6.95
ISBN 1 85224 500 X

ANTHONY DUNN

Pilots and Navigators

Oxford £6.99
ISBN 0 19 288095 0

CHRIS GREENHALGH

Of Love, Death and the Sea-Squirt

Bloodaxe £6.95
ISBN 1 85224 485 2

JUSTIN QUINN

Privacy

Carcanet £6.95
ISBN 1 85754 416 1

JULIE O'CALLAGHAN

No Can Do

Bloodaxe £7.95
ISBN 1 85224 511 5

AT 38 PAGES, Colette Bryce's debut collection *The Heel of Bernadette* feels somewhat underweight for £6.99, but maybe Picador are trying to nudge us back to the bad old days when slim over-priced volumes of verse were *de rigueur*. Nevertheless, Bryce's confident voice may prove worth the purchase for some readers. She has an interesting mixture of styles, ranging from the Hopkinesque in poems like 'Departure, Spanish Irish Time' –

All night we've breathed and breathed the minutes
in and out, our bones unfurled
in flat out lines like the times of our births

– to postmodern colloquialisms, demonstrated by some tongue-in-cheek titles: 'Hit Shite and It Flies High', 'Woman & Turkey' and 'Plot Summary, Scene 4'. Yet despite the brevity of this collection, and frequent startling highlights like her marvellous throwaway in 'Itch' – "I believe that Jesus lives / deep in the ditch of my mother's ear" – Bryce could still have jettisoned quite a handful of these first poems in favour of later work. The Lewis Carroll-influenced 'Epilogue', describing an accident in a car driven by "menstrual, resentful"Alice, is one example of a poem which plainly fails to pull its weight, lacking any good reason for its inclusion besides a heavy reliance on white rabbit humour. I must repeat here my apparently controversial belief that publishing too soon does nobody any favours, least of all a poet whose work is so clearly earmarked for future prominence.

One of the essential flavours of Bryce's work is a leaning towards song lyric style, though this is not always reflected in over-simplicity. She has a talent for capturing a mood through the use of imagistic anecdote, as in the nostalgic 'Father, in the face', where she focuses the poem's retreat into memory by invoking "the strange stopped nature of the day" as seen through a pair of binoculars. Easy shifts in rhythm and a subtle use of rhyme both contribute to a poem which lingers pleasingly in the memory.

Colette Bryce's strengths include an impressive unwillingness to be pigeonholed into any one particular style, and a realisation that poetry can only reach its true potential under tension.

Polly Clark

Polly Clark's debut collection *Kiss* rightly earned her a Poetry Book Society Recommendation. Canadian-born but brought up in England, Clark reflects her mixed origins by possessing an unusual and somewhat compelling turn of phrase in these poems, which shape-shift through multiple personalities as their maker grows in confidence. Her experience of working in a zoo has clearly paid dividends: coupled with an eye for minute detail, her descriptions of animals are always subtly linked to the world outside their cages.

In other words, hers is not first and foremost "nature" poetry; rather like a box of photographs, this collection is also peopled with glimpses of human relationships past, present and even future. But rather than being unrelated glimpses, everything eventually connects back to the source: in fact, Clark often appears to be sorting through them merely in order to establish a firmer hold on her own identity, as in the curiously terse 'Flowers', where "He kisses me among the selves / that never made it this far".

As is to be expected from a first collection,

however, there are moments of weakness that might have been better held back in favour of later work. 'Progress Diary', a poem of bereavement, was an ambitious technical idea from the school of Bridget Jones, but one whose lightweight tone necessarily fails to contain and control such a powerful emotion as grief: "Comfort 0 people. Shed (approx) 3 tears". In the same vein, whenever Clark retreats into a purely anecdotal poetry, she seems to lose sight of that musicality her more personally-engaged poems possess in abundance. One of the stronger poems in this first collection is 'My Life with Horses', where she reluctantly identifies with the instinctual side of nature – "I'm trying to hide the animal I am" – in a way that makes the poem merge brilliantly with its subject.

Amanda Dalton

Although *How to Disappear* is a first full-length collection, Amanda Dalton is no newcomer to the poetry world. A former director at the Arvon Foundation's Lumb Bank centre, she has been publishing her poetry in magazines and pamphlets for some years and has already developed a strong and self-assured poetic voice. Adept at the currently much-favoured nostalgic tone, Dalton's poems possess a muscularity which usually expresses itself through a bold choice of verbs and adjectives, so that no opportunity for impact is wasted. This muscularity sometimes works against itself, however, resulting in a dazzling overload of sound and imagery, but luckily more sparingly written pieces also exist alongside that verbal daring, achieving an overall balance of sorts.

With a distinct feel of the Northern school, this is poetry with its sleeves rolled up. The direct colloquialism of a poem like 'Strong Hands' is representative of her best style. Written from a male point of view, its barely controlled anger delivers a verbal punch to the throat, reflecting Dalton's natural confidence with "character" poems:

> See. Strong hands.
> I stink like an old dog fox
> but I'm good as any man.

A basically theatrical poet, she thoughtfully adapts her tone in these poems to the voice of each character, but is also unafraid to expose herself as a narrator at times. In one of her more personal poems, 'This House', Dalton slowly develops a wonderfully atmospheric imagery which raises the hairs on the back of the neck:

> But it wasn't enough
> so I began to eat this house.
>
> At first I gagged on the thin white walls
> and grazed my throat on an edge of light
> at the bedroom door...

Where she occasionally fails, as with Polly Clark, it is usually down to a sudden and unnecessary loss of musicality. One of Dalton's weaker poems is 'The Gifts' where her somewhat over-cluttered lines seem to reflect a basic confusion of motive in writing the poem in the first place:

> You told me that I'd landed on your doorstep
> like a totally inexplicable delivery
> of laminated knitting patterns,
> handed you a piping hot tripe supper
> and a Co-op bag of dog-eared Mills & Boons.

Whichever direction she eventually takes, Amanda Dalton already possesses a powerful ability to write which makes *How To Disappear* a worthwhile and often illuminating first collection.

Anthony Dunn

Possessed of an often unique voice, Anthony Dunn's first collection *Pilots and Navigators* is undoubtedly a showcase for an interesting new talent. For a poet still under thirty, Dunn has a powerful and accurate gift for rhythm; there is an almost physical insistence to his line-breaks that drags the reader's eye compulsively through each poem. Constantly aware of the possibilities of sound-patterns, he also produces delightfully playful lines like "Beyond our fleshy light all is haunted" and "You do not romanticize, / can see Welsh hills from Chester", designed to exercise the tongue as much as the mind.

If Dunn has a technical problem, it might be an occasional tendency to over-qualify. In 'Something to Say', I came across eight adjectives, which seems a tad excessive for a poem of only nine lines unless irony was intended. Which it may have been, since they seem so deliberately at odds with their subject:

> Wishing our van would wing up and after
> the ridiculous sunset,
> I held fast to the dangerous wheel, listening.

But there are other poems here that catch the eye unawares, usually through astonishingly delicate one-liners, like his throwaway description of tadpoles in a bucket, evolving "Limb by lung, quietly".

Dunn's innate understanding of the line-break, and indeed of rhythm itself, is what gives this first collection its curious power. As usual when dealing with a good writer, it's hard to give examples piecemeal; a reader ideally needs to see the whole in order to appreciate the intelligence behind its structure. But these poems are subtle, thought-provoking and yet enormously readable at the same time: how often can a critic say that of a first collection? Perhaps it's best to leave the poetry itself to finish this review, with the closing lines of 'What We Remember' acting as a sort of metaphor for Dunn's style:

> Three bombs have since exploded
> in places I have just left
> the narrowness of my escapes as fluid as fabled fish
> which never yet took offered bait.

Chris Greenhalgh

Open Chris Greenhalgh's second collection at any page and you will soon discover the strange delights of his often impossible imagery: "An unassimilated bit of tanning lotion / glistens on your belly like an iota of solar spit" ('The Fan'). What is "solar spit"? And does it matter? I know precisely what he means without being able to explain the analogy. Such moments of ambiguity coupled with startling accuracy permeate *Of Love, Death and the Sea-Squirt*, the collection's ironic title reflecting Greenhalgh's penchant for the curious and the unexpected, both in terms of imagery and subject matter.

The opening poem, 'A Short History of Milk' – in which a milk bath turns rather bizarrely into butter – demonstrates all that is admirable about this poet's work: anecdotal in tone, yet linguistically sensuous, unafraid of the unusual word in an incongruous position, and always revelling in the ironic:

> I pressed you between the thin
> white sheets of the bed, where you lay
> sheathed like a soft cheese in muslin:
> supple, mature, pungent; bright like the Milky Way.

His use of form is rarely as overtly rhymed as that

example, though. In many of these poems, his rhymes are subtle and almost organic in the way they spring naturally from the sense; the trademark of a master craftsman. A later poem, 'Gift', describes the discovery of a perfectly-fitting left plimsoll on a beach:

> And like the oar which seems broken in water
> then instantly heals as you lift it clear,
> I see the light – a fantasised sibling
> losing his footing
> and sending this sign
> across the ocean

Greenhalgh particularly enjoys putting human relationships under the microscope of language, and reproduces their minute tensions and comic moments extremely well: "...The word 'marriage' was broached / with the deft solemnity of a man handling high-grade uranium" ('My Funny Valentine'). But when a romantic poem finds itself the wrong side of serious, which only happens rarely, it does strike the odd discordant note in an otherwise original collection, as in 'The Last Seduction': "She cries as only a woman who believes in sin can cry".

At his comic best when observing the world from an ironic distance, Greenhalgh regularly produces hilarious image-combinations like "our great white Queen / watching the War Lords / in their ostentatious penis-gourds" ('Staying Alive'). I only hope that the six year gap between *Stealing the Mona Lisa* and *Of Love, Death and the Sea-Squirt* does not indicate another long wait for his next collection.

Justin Quinn

A poet of a completely different order to Greenhalgh, Justin Quinn writes with a prose-like deliberation which demands and often rewards close reading. Colloquial in tone yet coolly intellectual at the same time, his work in this second collection, *Privacy*, describes the world and its occupants with a conscientious eye for the "telling detail", dipping in and out of conversations and lives and ideas in order to do so.

Nevertheless, I was never quite convinced by the reality of nor the need for some of these poems. Poems should be written out of a sense of true urgency. But like those of Quinn's poems which fail to describe their world adequately, I failed to be drawn into that world simply because I could not see why it existed. A brief poem like 'Greeting' serves as an example:

> We'd just be swinging round on Pearse Street into
> > work
> When I'd look up occasionally and see your window:
> The wildest coloured cloths hung out and waved in
> > answer.

I see the intended picture, but if there was a good reason for creating it, I have missed the point of this poem entirely.

This is not to say that I found this collection uneventful. There are moments here of sheer genius, but they do seem to come more readily to Quinn when he abandons his tendency towards a prosiness that comes across poorly on the page. In 'Childishness' however, a wonderfully mythological slant coupled with a more loosely flowing form bring the poetry instantly to life:

> DREAM-FATHER: Wind,
> It's only wind, which these shapes can withhold.
> I know, for once I wound
> Them tight about myself, my lovers, my world

Another brilliantly sensuous touch, in his short-lined poem 'Insomnia', finds Quinn "swimming through / Myself as through / A kind of dark / Marvellous honey". Here form and language work beautifully together, conjuring up this magical atmosphere of introspection.

Julie O'Callaghan

Julie O'Callaghan's latest collection *No Can Do* is a book of three parts, all very different and unequal in strength. Following the lovely Japanese-inspired opening sequence of poems, the lengthy middle section contains some loose and often mystifyingly pointless single pieces, but the collection is saved by its strong elegiac finish, in an unsentimental and brutally honest exploration of her father's death which shows O'Callaghan writing at her very best.

Set in the court of Heian Japan, the opening sequence of poems is an absolute delight to read: satirically humorous, sparingly written, yet abundant in beautiful and sensuous images in miniature. One of her shorter pieces, 'Paper Shortage', encapsulates O'Callaghan's understated style in this sequence rather well:

> Don't make excuses
> about how difficult it is
> to find a sheet
> of delicate red-tinted Chinese paper.

Send a message
on a flat white pebble
or the stem of a hollyhock.
Etch your words
on a purple lotus petal.

By contrast, the middle section of *No Can Do* is cynical rather than satirical, its style urban and brashly colloquial to the point where the poetry itself fails to keep pace with O'Callaghan's desire to do justice to the modern world in which she lives. It is an admirable wish, to write poetry in the language of the everyday world, but I have always felt it to be a difficult balance to achieve. Although no doubt amusing in performance, lines like "There goes my watch alarm. / Time for a whacky round / of exec-

utive whirlyball" leave me rather cold on the page.

The third part of this collection, dedicated to her father's memory, shows a return to that more sparing style which kicked off *No Can Do* with such aplomb. Strong emotion seems to demand fewer words in poetry, and even those are always chosen with painstaking care. Understatement is clearly the order of the day in these elegiac poems: "sitting around / the chemotherapy room / for hours / I read all the magazines – twice / listening to the others / talk about the price of wigs".

Elegy does not always turn out well for less experienced poets, but O'Callaghan's technical expertise has undoubtedly helped her produce this moving sequence. Its clarity and honesty make her latest collection even more memorable after its impressive Japanese opening.

Minor Magic

by Matt Holland

JORGE LUIS BORGES

Selected Poems

Ed. Alexander Coleman
Allen Lane/The Penguin Press, £25
ISBN 0 713 99270 0

POETS WHO WRITE a lot and read little should visit the book-bound world of Borges. His writing would remind them of the importance of a literary apprenticeship, the value of literary heritage, and the limitations of language. He might also frighten them, put them off the profession, with his layered world of words, and still more words.

Jorge Luis Borges (1889–1986) man of mazes, mirrors, and all things labyrinthine, led a life so deep within the world of books that he seemed hardly able to find his way out. He says as much. "Little has happened in my life, but I have read a great deal". But at least he liked life in his tower of Babel and his reflections on language at work and play are invaluable to anyone interested in the art of writing well. He is one of those writers who not only demonstrates, by style alone, that language is a precision instrument and that we are duty bound to attempt to use it well, but also that he knows that life's chief complexities are far less utterable in words than many people would have us believe.

By way of explaining this, and innumerable other difficulties of language, literature, and life, most of Borges' collections of poetry have prose prologues, prefaces, and inscriptions, which are wonderfully wordy, exploratory, and explanatory in a way that British slim-volume introductions generally are not. For example, take this Inscription, which precedes an even longer Prologue, from his 1985 collection *Los Conjurados* ('The Conspirators')."To write a poem is to attempt a minor magic. The instrument of that magic, language, is mysterious enough. We know nothing of its origin. We know only that it divides into diverse lexicons and that each one of them comprises an indefinite and changing vocabulary and an undefined number of syntactic possibilities. With those evasive elements I have formed this book. (In the poem, the cadence and atmosphere of a word can weigh more than its meaning.)"

Now any poet who does not already know all this, is likely to be a sincere but superficial sentimentalist novice, but the rest among the best *PR* readers can still benefit from reminders like these. In fact, if readers are anything like this reviewer, they may even enjoy the prose bits as much as the poems, especially when they are inverted assertions like this: "Literature starts out from poetry and can take centuries to arrive at the possibility of prose. After four hundred years, the Anglo-Saxons left behind a poetry which was not just occasionally admirable and a prose which was scarcely explicit".

But what about the man's poems, in this new bilingual parallel Spanish-English text made up of thirteen collections dating from 1923 to 1985 and comprising 477 rough-trimmed pages of poems, as he says, often "scribbled out of boredom, negligence, and my own passions?" Well, for a start, many of them have rather huge, prosaic, and extended titles, like these: 'Manuscript Found in a Book of Joseph Conrad', 'Embarking on the Study of Anglo-Saxon Grammar'. Not the sort of titles to get you excited when the late summer sun is shining, tennis courts beckon, or Big Brother's on the box. And certainly not the kind of thing you expect out of South America, and more especially Argentina, where at least one popular poetic tradition was that of Martin Fierro, a narrative poem of epic proportion, by Jose Hernandez, that tells of a guerrilla gaucho's exploits on the pampas that included fighting wild Indians, lassooing wild cattle, wooing wild women, and getting drunk. Actually, Borges was so impressed by this poem, which he saw as a symbol of lost freedom, that he wrote two short stories on the Fierro cycle. There are also a couple of poems in this selection that nod in the direction of rural parts of the author's homeland. One of these, 'General Quiroga Rides to His Death in a Carriage', contains some of the chief failings of translations, especially super-academic ones, like these. It chooses the word "countryside", that evokes something kind and cultivated, for the original *campo,* which is wild and open; the prosaic and clumsy "stake for tethering beasts to" for the rhythmic and neat *estaca pampa*; and four-word "winds from the southwest" for the original's single-word *pampero*. As ever, translators do their best (where would single-language speakers be without them?) but they can do little more than capture meaning, and miss the music and native feel of the original. (And in this case, when they do go to the Spanish, in a footnote, they erroneously call a provincial tyrant of the pampas ['caudillo'] *candillo*.)

But since Borges, with an English grandmother, an ambitious city-dwelling lawyer for a father, a posh private secondary Swiss education, and youthful years spent reading English authors such as Chesterton, Stevenson, De Quincey, and Wilde, was definitely not a gaucho, it is not surprising that the body of his poetic work has a flavour that is far more English-European than it is South American. This should be a pleasure for the English reader, in both his poetry and prose. In 'The Other Tiger', readers can have a real Ted Hughes–Thought Fox trip, but with a striped wild animal of the jungle, as the poet imagines "the tiger I am calling up in my poem / a tiger made of symbols and of shadows, / a set of literary images".

In 'Happiness', a fine poem about key experiences and seeing things afresh, Borges calls up images that will be perfectly familiar to the cultivated northern-hemisphere reader, even if they now find something slightly unsettling about the line "Whoever looks at the ocean sees England". In solid literary-philosophical western tradition, Borges also likes to ask questions, especially rhetorical ones. In his awe-struck poem '1971', the opening lines pull you in. "Two men walked on the surface [no surface in the Spanish] of the moon. / Others will later. What are words to do? / And what of the dreams and fashionings of art / before this real, almost unreal, event?" In 'Anticipation of Love', there is a familiar but not quite comfortable mix of archaic English simile ("your brow fair as a feast day") and far-fetched New Age metaphor ("I shall discern that ultimate beach of your being"). Even though this floral style is less irritating in the Spanish, we can't blame the translators for everything.

Borges' phenomenal philosophical philandering is entirely his own. It is perhaps both his strength and his chief weakness. Maybe he was something like the Jesuit Baltasar Gracian, whose name is the title of a poem that reflects on a life locked in language. A life of "Labyrinths, symbols . . . / a cold and overintricate nothingness/ . . . . a vain / herbal of metaphors and sophistries". Certainly, what is noticeable about this collection of poems, spanning sixty years, are the many layers of language at work, the rich veins of ideas, and curiously, the poet's own name featuring more than any one else's. But that is not a problem. By the time you have read the entire collection, Borges and I ("the other Borges is the one things happen to") will have become Borges and you.

Matt Holland writes:
During the last twenty years, I have led reading groups for the external studies department of the universities of Oxford and Bristol, as well as independently organised but generally more dynamic ones in backwaters of Wiltshire and Gloucestershire. Whether doing poetry or prose I *always* start sessions by reading a poem aloud, usually by a living poet. I do this for three reasons. To get participants out of general chit-chat mode and into a text and literary mood; to introduce them to more contemporary poetry, and to encourage the practice of reading a poem and listening. Many people react favourably to poems introduced like this and acknowledge that they tend not to discover them on their own. I am about to start a new reading group in Swindon.

Sensual Consciousness

by Tom Fulton

SHARON OLDS

Blood, Tin, Straw

Cape, £8.99

ISBN 0 224 06089 9

I DISCOVERED SHARON OLDS while reading the anthology *The Rag and Bone Shop of the Heart*. I followed this up with *Satan Says* and *The Dead and the Living*, both published in the early 1980s. In these collections, Olds' poetry combines sensuous, keenly observed images with searing emotion in a way that achieves a trance-inducing intensity. The poetry was often grounded in personal family experiences which included, during her childhood, shuddering, shattering incidents of abuse. The poems were blunt, edgy, and earthy, but also subtle, exploring many dimensions of family experience over several generations. Perhaps most of all, Olds demonstrated an admirable capacity to blend both rage and understanding, an ability to move through without forgetting. She seemed like an artist unusually alert to the complexity of evil, but neither detached from its horror, nor immobilized.

Sharon Olds' poetry can be viewed as a guided tour of a world neglected or repressed in modern culture – a world that's alien, intriguing and seductive. This world is the intermediate realm in a tripartite universe, located between spirit and body, that the archetypal psychologist James Hillman describes as the world of soul, the *anima mundi*, where all matter is alive and vibrant with soul qualities. Poetry so boldly faithful to this world is an artistic and political statement.

I looked forward to reading Olds' latest work, *Blood, Tin, Straw* to see how her perspectives might have evolved since *Satan Says* and *The Dead and the Living*. I was disappointed. The images in her earlier works seemed more democratic and accessible; the story lines were clearer and more compelling. *Blood, Tin, Straw* often seemed oblique and inaccessible. Occasionally the language felt gratuitously graphic, less courageous than sensational. The allusions were frequently private and obscure, and some poems,

most notably 'What is the Earth?' seemed poetically self-conscious wordplay. Yet, there was still much to admire and appreciate. The work reminded me of atonal classical music – discordant, fragmented, but with bursts of breathtaking melodies.

Olds' sustained emotional intensity is announced like a fanfare with the first poem in the book, 'The Promise,' in which she and, presumably, her husband, promise to kill each other if illness renders them not "able to think or die":

> With the second drink, at the restaurant,
> holding hands on the bare table,
> we are at it again, renewing our promise
> to kill each other...

This intensity dances with an ability to perceive infinity in a single event, even a single moment and to communicate from inside life experiences, rather than from above. Olds explores her personal memories with imagination, creativity, and a relentlessly sensual consciousness, as in this recollection of her newborn child in 'The New Stranger':

> No one has known my ignorance so well, so
> smelled my fear, there, with the fresh
> abundant milk...
>
>   ...I didn't exist
> until you smiled at me, and in your
> brilliant loam-colored iris I saw,
> tiny as an embryo,
> your mother smile.

This ability to perceive so much in a single detail seems most fully realized when Olds writes about the many dimensions of love and marriage as they come together in sex. In language that is both graphic and tender, Olds recreates sexual experience as a synthesis of spirit, emotion, and lust, as in the poem 'At Home':

> ...He naps, but I do not
> want to let him go, I feel
> delicious, remembering desire, the ways
> he increased and increased it. His eyelid lifts –
> justice, mercy. We look at each other
> till our eyes are wet, then we rest awhile,
> and then we stare are each other, almost
> emotionless with sex and trust.

Also evident in *Blood, Tin, Straw* is the sensuality of a body fully present and open to the natural environment, as in 'Outdoor Shower':

> ... Now open your eyes –
> green lawn, silver pond,
> grey dune, blue Atlantic,
> the simple fields of God, liquid and solid.
> Turn and turn in hot water,
> column of heat in the cool wind
> and sunny air, squeeze your eyes and then
> open them again – look, it is still there,
> the world as heaven, your body on the edge of it.

In *Blood, Tin, Straw* one finds Olds' familiar themes of family pain and dysfunction, which seem somehow sanctified by an awareness of her own dark shadow, revealed in such poems as 'Warrior: 5th Grade', 'Poem to the Reader', and the 'Spouses Waking Up in the Hotel Mirror'. Also, there is the relentless self-disclosure which is characteristic of her work, the courage to be visibly vulnerable, which seems paradoxical, in the sense that it evokes both admiration and curiosity. One wonders if there are mysteries and secrets concealed amidst so much honesty.

Of all the poems in *Blood, Tin, Straw*, I found 'The Knowing' – the last poem in the book – the most moving: a tender love poem in the best sense of the term. It was a wonderful climax and counterpoint to the first poem in the collection:

> ... we lie a long time
> looking at each other.

I do not know what he sees, but I see
eyes of quiet evenness
and endurance, a patience like the dignity
of matter...

By knowing him, I get to know
the purity of the animal
which mates for life. Sometimes he is slightly
smiling, but mostly he just gazes at me gazing,
his entire face lit...

When I wake again, he is still looking at me,
as if he is eternal.

Although the poems in *Blood, Tin, Straw* were less resonant to me than her earlier works, Olds remains for me an admirably serious woman who knows her way around both the visible and the hidden world, and can hold the tension between the two.

Tom Fulton writes:

I fell in love with poetry 10 years ago when I heard an audio tape of Coleman Banks and Robert Bly reading the poems of Rumi, the Sufi mystic. Some other poets I enjoy are William Blake, Kabir, Mary Oliver, Rilke, Antonio Machado. For me, poetry is a very sensate experience and a poem doesn't really penetrate until I read it aloud. For the last 20 years I have worked as the President of a non-profit organisation that supports programs to alleviate poverty and homelessness. I believe that the long term solution to social ills is to balance our usual rational, analytical approaches with poetic, psychological and artistic perspectives.

Modest Recording Angel

By Guy Wareing

U. A. FANTHORPE

Consequences

Peterloo Poets, £7.95
ISBN 1 871471 83 4

THE POETRY OF U. A. Fanthorpe has always been a pleasure to read aloud. For those of us who make it a habit this new collection of poems will be a particular pleasure. She has an ability to engage in conversations with the reader and her audience in a way that seems simple and direct. This creates an illusive simplicity which hides a much deeper, darker voice.

The first section of the book comprises thirteen linked poems entitled 'Consequences' which are "about, among other things, England and Leicestershire and Richard III, and hope, courage and gypsies ... The title (the name of an old party-game) suggests that nothing happens in isolation from the past or the future". U. A. Fanthorpe has always ranged widely in time and space and in this sequence we move from the flag on the front cover of the Battle of Bosworth through to 'The Young Person's Guide to Arms' with its encouraging "newspeak" definitions:

Collateral Damage. This is when Children and

Ordinary People come between enemies and get killed. It's really their fault for being in the wrong place at the wrong time.

Her deceptively light touch probes the nerve and she is prepared to confront the alien in us: "We each inherit our shadow, our ration of darkness". Her words are always honest and she, more than many, will have no truck with "a disinfected vocabulary". She is, we feel, a friend of "Children and Ordinary People" but not an uncritical admirer. This poem sequence says more about England now and our choices than a lorry load of political manifestos from any party.

One of her great gifts is to take a landscape, a picture or a poem and tell us what the occupants are thinking and feeling. In 'Maud Speaking' she, as Maud, sets about Tennyson with enthusiasm, and others in the literary world get a friendly thump or two. In 'Overheard at Lumb Bank (two tutors consult)' Wordsworth is warned off from talking too much to children.

You'd better watch it Bill, I said to him.
I'd rather you stuck to daffodils while you're here.

Her range encompasses the concerns of the ordinary people which are seen in an extraordinary way. Her friend Olive, a cleaner in the hospital at Bristol, is linked to Athene, "the wise goddess, who presented Athens with the olive tree, the gift most useful to mortals". Olive gave U. A. Fanthorpe the gifts of food, drink, laughter and lilies and is immortalised in her poem. (I heard her read 'Olive' as a two hander with a friend at last year's Cheltenham Literature Festival and re-reading it is like coming home to someone you already know.)

The explanatory footnotes are sometimes a little eccentric. At times they are hugely helpful and at others they seem a trifle perverse. At one point during the reading of the poems I found myself with her small book of poetry and an Atlas of Great Britain, *The Shorter Oxford Dictionary*, *The Dictionary of Quotations*, flower books, modern painting books and (for some good reason) *The Place Names of Cumbria*. She has a wide range of reference and sometimes chooses to explain it but most often not. I am still looking for a reference to 'SO 759934:14.2.96. A Love Poem', although I suspect it is to do with the Forest of Dean, but footnote was there none. This is not a particularly vehement criticism as we all like a little mystery and I

am made more anxious to visit The Burren on the West Coast of Ireland – "Bloody-minded sort of place" – after reading her poem about it. The first of the poems which I have read aloud in reality, rather than in the mind's ear, is called 'Postcards'. Here the throwaway clichés of everyday communication are held up for view, teased and cherished with "the walkabout postman" wondering and decoding, as far as he can, the enigmatic messages. This could have been left as a vignette about the difficulties of using words to speak to each other as many have done ("I gotta use words when I talk to you") but U.A Fanthorpe makes her own angle to the universe plain to us in the final lines:

Look in the graveyard, as you make your round;
There are the ultimate postcards, trite as ever,
Stylised as runes, with a subtext intricate

As a crossword puzzle clue, or house-agents blurb,
Delivering the last message of stay at homes
To those who have left on a journey beyond
                                    deliveries:

Gone, not forgotten; Sadly missed; Wish you were here.

U.A. Fanthorpe makes us freshly see and taste old things. Her often laconic humour seduces us into missing at first the place where "A dog is finding something beastly to eat / Under a hawthorn". She sees these dark places with pity and no fear. She is to be found (with the charladies in 'Afterwards') "down on our hands and knees, / Laughing, and mopping up".

She is a modest recording angel who sketches pictures of our human condition with an economical line. Her voices speak to us about ourselves and we know ourselves better after hearing them.

Guy Wareing writes:
My monthly engagement is with a roving Cotswolds poetry reading group. The host sets a theme in advance and provides the supper. The numbers vary from eight to sixteen and we read in turn. We hear some thirty to forty poems in an evening and usually bring twice that number. Our ability to listen has improved over the fifteen years we have been in existence. The choice as to what to read as your turn arrives makes for good creative tension. To continue the theme or counterpoint it? How to change the tone? Can you repeat your favourite poem if someone has already read it? Your choice. Do it. But, please, let the poem speak for you, don't analyse it, read us another poem.

The Geoffrey Dearmer Prize

The Geoffrey Dearmer prize was instigated in 1997 in honour of the noted WWI poet and the Poetry Society's oldest member, Geoffrey Dearmer, who died in 1996. The first award was won by Paul Farley and the second by Sarah Wardle. Thanks to a generous bequest by Geoffrey Dearmer's family, the Prize is now awarded annually. This year's judge is Maura Dooley, and the Dearmer Prize winner will be featured in the Winter issue of *Poetry Review*.

THE SHORTLIST

JONATHAN TREITEL

I WAS BORN in London, and studied poetry with Denise Levertov in California. My poems have appeared in *Poetry Review, Ambit, London Magazine, Jewish Quarterly, Jerusalem Review*. Recently I have lived part of the year in Jerusalem and New York.

TWO POEMS BY JONATHAN TREITEL
THE GREAT EUROPEAN POEM

Some kilometres ago I read the Great European Poem.
Misremembered quite where.
Daubed on a cave-wall?
Neither up nor down an Alpine pass, having clomped a good way on
　　　　　　　　　　　　　　　　　　　　its elephant-feet?
Lost-and-not-yet-found in the Channel tunnel?
On a Viking funeral-pyre, all its stanzas ablaze, halfway up the Volga?
Syllables of it still twinkle at low tide.
Chinking fragments crawl to the surface, where they shouldn't be, by
　　　　　　　　　　　　　　　　　　　　　　　rights.

But there you have it.
Even its language is neither here nor there. "Do you speak
　　　　　　　　　　　　　　　　　　Europeanish?"
They say it retreated from Moscow with snow on its line-breaks.
An after-rhyme twitched a dew-web in a copse in Pomerania.
Nothing left of it now, except an ache in a phantom verse,
and a stench of burning.

COLOURING IN THE CALENDAR

Monday: blue. Like the blueing that goes in the wash, that comes out in
the wash. The laundry finally the color it always was. Blue that
simply makes white whiter.

Tuesday: green. Grass-green. A field of grass. You walk all over it, what is it?
Oh just what it is.

Red Wednesday. Revolution from which verb? Revolt or revolve? Dawn or
sunset. The hours in between are for waiting. While-away
Wednesday. White or black between red and red.

Yellow Thursday. Gas flares through coal-smog. Historic Thursday smeared
with the remains of ancient, decayed Thursdays.

Friday: violet. Haze the summation of all the air between here and the
mountainside. Far-off Friday. Elsewhere the vulture's shadow flaps
across the mihrab.

Orange Saturday. A fruit of a day. Day we can sense with our eyes closed.
Even zest-less, it's still orange, admirable. Inhaled and gulped to
the last pip. Scents us.

Sunday: indigo? I suppose. Ach what else in the rainbow's left? Dyestuff
farmed for us by slaves in our colonies. Day of whose rest? Colour
we could do without. Oh bring on the pure clear blue of long-
forgotten Monday!

ANNA WIGLEY

I WAS BORN in Cardiff in 1962, and have lived here ever since, except for a student year in London. My family was fairly unconventional, and I grew up surrounded by the animals and birds my brothers kept in large numbers. The elder brother kept predatory birds; at one point we had a Peregrine falcon tethered to a perch in the back garden. I went to a convent school though our family were not Catholics. When I left school I went to college, dropped out, and had the usual mixture of picturesque and dead-end jobs: I worked in a Probate Registry, ushered at two theatres, was a bookshop assistant, waitress, and, briefly, an army barracks dishwasher. Aged 25 I returned to college, studied English, then went on to do a Ph.D on Iris Murdoch's novels. I started getting poems published in the small magazines in 1996. Now I write fiction reviews for my local paper, *The Western Mail*, and, occasionally, poetry reviews for Welsh magazines. I'm hoping to have a first poetry collection published before too long. The poets I most admire and reread are what I would call natural rhapsodists: Ted Hughes, Norman MacCaig, Rilke, Michael Longley, and Jeremy Hooker.

TWO POEMS BY ANNA WIGLEY
THE SONGBIRDS

Exiles from a vanished world
of intricate brightness; escapees
from the last Book of Hours,
where they woke to skies of unpolluted blue
and dived through them like angel fish,

these silk-embroidered birds
unspool from tiny throats
their gold and vermillion threads.
More swiftly than the petrol sheen
from their feathers widens the eye,
the song goes up,

an instantaneous tapestry minutely worked
with colours cool as mercury,
and hot as molten brass.

So delicate, a hand's embrace
could snuff the guttering candle of the heart
in its eggshell case,

so finished in each detail, a crest
might serve for Thumbelina's fan,

they quiver for a second
on the edges of our world
like momentary effects of light.

BOXING DAY TO LIDNEY

After the night's slow
tempera of crystal and flake

laying layers of silence
white on white,

the valley is painted
at shoulder and hip:

a voluptuously sequinned
starlet in Versace.

The quiet has gathered
on the paw-pads of firs,

sprayed stones with salt,
left grassblades sugared,

laid a line of white
on the meanest twig.

By dawn the birches
are sculptures of ice,

silver-scarved necks
rustling heads of lace.

The fields are white lakes
of coconut milk

below an acre of blue
with the lid blown off.

Under the trees at noon
shadows lay small black knives.

JOHN STAMMERS

I AM A previous editor of *Magma* poetry magazine. I write interviews with poets for *Magma* and *Poetry London*. My first collection *Panoramic Lounge-bar* will be published by Picador in March 2001. I am an Associate of King's College, London and live in Islington where I was born.

TWO POEMS BY JOHN STAMMERS
CERTAIN SUNDRY MATTERS

for M.A.M

Inasmuch as you have ever heard a cowbell
extol the mountains that roll under the cow
that's wearing it, then the morning I most readily recall
was on the *Col d'Aubisque*, the mist in the valleys
like pale milk vapour from the *café complet*
we hadn't had and undulating through them
and over the ungulates,

whereas we, being right at the top then,
or over it possibly, when we came to a stop
on the apron of gravel that spread itself out
onto the roadway, and was not like an apron
at all really, in front of the old Aubèrge
from which that girl recited *Le petit déjeuner* for us,
her smile as sweet as apricot preserve
in the morning, then you too may recall
the butter, absolutely white without salt,
was a single marble bar,

so that the sawry knives scored lines on it,
back and forth, and yearned for something to divert them
from the ruts they themselves made, poor knives
born, when hot, to slide through it like lovers
go through their days, but, being cold and all,
only able to scrape the surface,

so that nonetheless the air itself
was invisible as usual, but I longed
to feel it's hands again on my face in a caress;
so that I said "The hills are alive
with the sound of mooing";
so that "John, don't be a bloody fool"; you said,

and given that her *petit ami* burped up on his velo,
de rigueur on that eructating conveyance,
his red foulard *de trop*, I thought, at his throat,
and that if it all could have been just a bit more *noir*,
or *nouvelle vague* even, we might at least
have essayed to stay up there;
and that not being the case we bid them
the long *au revoir*, the atmosphere thin
and unable to sustain us any longer in those reaches;
we had come as far as we could,
or perhaps a little farther

and insofar as we started the road down together,
heading for the Horizon
(which was the car not the sierra,
which was the mountains not the car)
and it took us these years to get down from there,

thereby did we arrive separately.

WEATHER REPORT

Sea Vista fluoresces like luminous eels;
someone painted this place cream
and never touched it again.
You can't get that colour anymore,
just cream, you say;
flakes detach from the facade
and join in the general descent.

The tint of the rain drops' perpetual concerto
misses, by about none,
the lilac of the waltzes of the tea room.
So much liquid, is it all required?
Take cappuccino or lip gloss,

those suspensions of our age,
or the actual rain:
clouds (mauve semblance of what is)
accumulate as if instructed by old masters.
And when you think about it, El Greco's wrist
did live its life inches from the very threshold of creation,
the canvases like culture mediums,
spread with florets of grim hues and him
drawing out the grand designs into being
through the tip of the brush.

And as if to prove conclusively
that there is madness in Methodism,
the sign outside the mock-gothic hail says:
In the Midst of Life we are in Death
but you, you wear the ludicrous sea-side hats
of self-aggrandisement, as if the gust
that tossed the last one into the sea
was your own idea: not content
with wrapping yourself up
in love, only love, love,
you do no more than write an epigraph for us
on the back of the old hotel
with its seen better days
and panoramic lounge-bar:

THEY CAME THEY SAW THEY CAME

Ha Ha Ha, you went.
Don't perpetrate mirth like that,
you spray-can El Greco,
I said, and I noticed
the soft flesh of your wrist
and wanted you again.

IVY GARLITZ

I was born in Miami and taught English as a foreign language in Poland and Germany before settling in Britain. I have recently completed a PhD in Creative and Critical Writing at the University of East Anglia. As well as being a featured poet in *Thumbscrew*, my poems have appeared in *Poetry Review*, the *Honest Ulsterman*, *The Rialto* and several other magazines. 'The Writer's Beginning' was overall winner of the Women's Hour sonnet competition and was broadcast on Radio 4. My pamphlet, *A Better Life*, is published by the Bay Press. I have recently returned from presenting academic papers at the international Comic Arts Conference in San Diego. I have a keen interest in writing for the internet; my webcam project was one of the winners of the Showcase competition for innovative websites featured on the BBC2's *The Net*.

TWO POEMS BY IVY GARLITZ
CANCELLED SOAP OPERA

Our options are at an end,
after all our struggles
with no network willing to pick us up

we're goners.
So we've gathered in our church
to marry our supercouple.

Our years of twisted plots
have been teased out
to our last hour:

no more mothers pulling strings,
ex-fiancées telling tales,
scheming best friends, or floozies on the make

can keep them apart any longer.
Let them clasp hands
before we vanish from the air,

the fabric of our sets unrolled,
the especially built palatial homes
prised into planks, this solemn mission,

our world itself
goes out with the lights.
Our assembled cast is clutching

the destined ones they've found
in time, so no one ends up alone,
and will beam

as our priest proclaims love is forever
and our leading man lifts the veil
of his bride, the one star

of our project which failed
to please enough;
even her tears

couldn't raise the numbers to keep us all
from getting canned.
Let's not recount now

the lies, the sicknesses, crashes, bombs,
the despicable driven out of town
for not stirring enough trouble

or sympathy for their victims.
We'll entertain our followers
with a kiss at fade out.

But please, before the credits have to run
and our theme played for the final time
give us, who acted out your fantasies,

a chance:
before the happy ending comes
which was never scripted to arrive,

grant us a sequence in which we can forget
our vendettas,
our fists raised for attention,

and just look at one another, unprovoked,
hold our babies snatched away
and those taken from us

much too early
without having to worry
what people will think.

Before we dissolve into happiness
everybody says they want to see
but no one wants to watch

let us trash our lines
and wing it –
indulge us a moment of life

plain
and full
in its predictable repetitiveness.

FIRST WOMAN ON THE MOON

There weren't only men on those missions
though twelve touched down and walked
commended by textbooks
and official patches.

I rode to the moon
on a cuff checklist
tucked in between lists for core samples
and bonus comments,

reminders to look
for surface irregularities
and scuff resistance.
I was unsuited,

naked to the elements,
my tits dangling,
with only a helmet of hair.
I rode back

to be left
in lockers alongside their chisels,
their cases for samples.
But I haven't greyed

like them, grown long past
those moments in vacuum.
I haven't had to force arthritic limbs
through tours and conventions,

giving interviews to inspire businessmen,
missing the tether on my back,
the blue marble floating, hanging
on my every word.

I straddle my flowered chair
hugging it
as I did while jumping craters
supported by NASA's arm,

unmonitored,
unflagged,
unfazed by gravity
or the lack of it.

MARTHA KAPOS

I WAS BORN in New Haven, Connecticut, and grew up in Cambridge, Massachusetts. I first came to London after finishing a degree in Classics at Harvard. My plan was to have a year abroad studying Painting and the History of Art at the Chelsea College of Art. I never went back, and I'm still at Chelsea where I now teach. It's curious that although I've been in London for most of my life now, my centre of gravity, in terms of poetry, is still in America: Stevens, Williams, and a number of contemporary Americans are the poets I most avidly read. I'm grateful to Chelsea for receiving the serial transformation of my identity – from painter to art historian to poet – with a good grace, and for allowing my teaching to follow suit. I have written two books on painting and poetry in early modernism. In 1989 The Many Press brought out a pamphlet, *The Boy Underwater* which was my first poetry publication. Since then, apart from *Poetry Review*, I've had poems in a number of anthologies and magazines including *Agenda, Poetry London, Thumbscrew, The Rialto* and the *TLS*. I received a Hawthornden fellowship in 1994. A first collection is in preparation.

TWO POEMS BY MARTHA KAPOS
THE NIGHT KITCHEN

Outside extinct stars hang
like scrunched-up letters thrown
around the floor. The earth is poised
on a hook above the sink.
An enormous sponge sits planetary and alone
in its enamel dish. So if I notice

a cracked glass face-down needs chucking out,
the draining-board is chipped by something
dropped last year, the forks all look
faintly yellow between their prongs,
why do my arms wrapped in mist in the Fairy liquid
feel the long warm pull of the tide,

why is it suddenly all
a darkness of islands in oceans, the inconstant soap
a slab of light slipping between my fingers
like a moon? And if the folded
dishcloth rises to a pinnacle of hope
against an embroidery of midnight-blue,

and if the bubbles coming on and going out
range themselves in a white ring big
as the Crab Nebula, and if I'm floating
inches above the ground, the pocket in my apron
growing into a pouch so large that it could hold
Medusa's head, J-cloths flapping

from my heels like the wings of Mercury,
and through the hazy half-dark I begin to see
a constellation in a drift of dust,
puddles on the floor big enough to hold the Milky Way,
will you keep the earth's poles

together between your firm hands, administer
the law of gravity, and hold onto all
the rattling atoms of the world?

PANTOMIME

Faces facing across the table,
this is when we lift the lid
off the box, take out the flat
brown suit, then gravely as a crown

loop the tunnel of the neck
over our heads, unroll the four
rumpled legs, step in and run the zip

up the stomach. This is better
than we thought: the bronze rump
shining in the sun, the velvet lips,
the curve of the intelligent neck.
Sit back and watch the perfect

half-wit smile spread. Swaying
gently like a milk-float
(to light applause) tiny
goose-steps locked

we tinker up onto the stage.
I spill a long wet tongue
from the mouth. You aim a graceful
squirt of milk from the penis

(a standing ovation) push
a spot-lit hand through to wag the tail.
Sausages are gliding in a pink heap
onto the floor. We paw the earth,

lower the dynamic head and take
several fences. Now we're floating
high over the steep hills and far away.
Yes it is. No it's not – a large

crumpled heap of corduroy on the floor.
Don't miss it. Our double act
zipped up together in the semi-dark,
heads I win, tails you lose,

is for this limited season only.
We collapse the legs, rub out
the eyes, take up the ears by the roots.
But hold on. The stable-door is locked.

This horse is a cuckoo
in the nest, a marching army of occupation,
an enormous tongue in the mouth.
It will run and run.

GRETA STODDART

BORN IN 1966 in Henley, I grew up in Belgium and Oxford. Having lived and studied in Paris I now live in London. I have won several prizes including 1st Prize in the 1998 Exeter Poetry Prize and 2nd Prize in the 1998 TLS/Blackwells Poetry Competition. My poems have appeared in *Poetry Review, The North, TLS, Independent on Sunday* and *Verse* (US). My work was included in *Paradise for Sale* – an anthology edited by Selima Hill and a selection will be published in the forthcoming Enitharmon anthology *Tying the Song*. I was awarded a Hawthornden International Fellowship in 1999 and am currently poetry tutor at Morley College in London.

TWO POEMS BY GRETA STODDART
UNREQUITED

As the stalker sets out on the route he knows by heart
and the climber starts to ascend the high and blinding snow
so the lover will up in the middle of the night, and go.

With only a star, or radio, for company
he finds peace on the road, to be moving at last.
Wipers jauntily clear the screen the better to see

the blackness ahead, and inside a thin stick
lurches round the calm green face of the clock
and a red needle trembles at its constancy.

There are things he meant to say but now at her door he turns
and sees his shadow stretch and stagger up the steps behind him
as if it bore the load of all the miles he'd covered:

the flooded fields, the black-eyed classrooms and mute estates,
all the Kings' Heads and hollow ways, the lit pane
of one who couldn't sleep. And standing there he knows

not why he came, but now he's come it's gone, and how
like the ignorant prey, love wants nothing of him
and what he took for a wave was a scrap of flag in the wind.

LA BERCEUSE

I once had the power to wake and terrify small children
including myself, by finding I was rocking to and fro,
banging my head against the pillow, and moaning
sounds my parents learnt to ignore as they sat and dozed,

I like to think, in front of David Attenborough,
that time he stalked the jungle and came across a chimp,
a baby one, alone in a clearing, his arms wrapped
like cord around him, rocking on his haunches, and whimpering.

Classic runt behaviour, cooed the narration,
pining for the arms of a mother grown weary of nursing, or dead.
But I've seen it too in wild prodigal children,
hugging the movement like a wound, and in men on the edge

of chairs beating the air in bright, stale rooms.
I've seen it in the standard loony in 'B' movies
and bad acting classes, in the bag lady
and men on their knees, bending, as if to drink, from the page.

Now, though rarer, it's enough to alarm a new lover
as I sit bolt upright, my crazed nest of hair.
It's not so much a long story, I say, *as one
without beginning or end, but it's nothing* but something

like the sway of woman, the shift from side to side
of donkey and swaddled load plodding along the tide,
the swing's slow subsidence now the child is out of sight,
the sleeper on track for Lethe pummeling the night.

NEWS/COMMENT

UPPING THE ANTE

The pressure to promote poetry that began in 1994 with New Generation Poets and the first National Poetry Day resulted in a series of initiatives each aiming to cap the other. The two big poetry book prizes – the Forward and the Eliot – are now vying with each other to put a few more poets into the VAT-rated league: next year, the Eliot Prize will be matching Forward's £10,000 prize. The shortlist goes up in November and the prize will be awarded in January 2001. Forward's response is awaited.

LEVIATHAN

Michael Hulse is one of the most committed and independent-minded poetry editors around. Flexing his muscles after *The New Poetry*, a stint as Arc's editor and his co-editorship of *Stand,* he is now launching a new poetry imprint, Leviathan. It promises a higher standard of production than is usual for poetry and the first three titles, published for National Poetry Day, are Kit Wright's *Hoping it Might be So: Poems 1974–2000*, Jackie Wills's *Party* and Roger Finch's *Fox in the Morning*. Finch is an American who, according to Michael Hulse is a "Proust writing in Marianne Moore stanzas". The act of bringing Kit Wright back into print by itself counts as a major service to poetry.

First collections by Giles Goodland and Stephanos Papadopoulos follow in March 2001 and the list also promises classics and poetry from India, Canada, Mexico, Cuba, Italy and the Netherlands alongside a core list of UK and US poetry.

ALDEBURGH FESTIVAL: 3-5 NOVEMBER

This year's is the twelfth Aldeburgh Poetry Festival and the winning formula remains the same: a long weekend – Friday to Sunday – of poets from the UK and abroad reading to large audiences. This year's innovation is a talk, by Michael Hofmann on his hero Robert Lowell. Poets include the American Thomas Lux and C. K. Williams, Julie O'Callaghan, the Slovenian Tomas Salamun, plus home-grown Roger McGough, U. A. Fanthorpe, and Graham Mort. Ruth Padel is conducting a masterclass on the Sunday.
Box Office: 01728 453543

NET VERSE

Boomerang is a smart new magazine of poetry and prose hitting cyberspace at **http://www.boomeranguk.com/** The poetry editor is Neil Rollinson, so it's not surprising that the 'zine is visually pretty stunning. Neil has succeeded in attracting poets more often associated with print than browser (such as Gerard Woodward, Matthew Sweeney and Penelope Shuttle) to the first edition. The magazine is hoping to publish animated poems as well as conventionally static work in the future. And speaking of the future, there's even a special version of the site, with short poems suitable for display on your WAP phone. Oh yes, it pays for contributions, too.

The name of (this) poetry site is a little confusing, but it can be found easily enough at **http://www.thispoetrysite.com/** It's an attractive magazine, and also provides its contents in Adobe Acrobat format for off-line browsing. This is a good thing and more magazine sites ought to consider it. The magazine itself is almost entirely poetry; no editorial, a bit of background, and links.

By contrast, Martin Blyth's site at **http://martinblyth.co.uk/** contains very little poetry, but a number of essays and letters on various aspects of the poetry scene. Martin has strongly held, and often controversial opinions. His entertaining and incisive account of the Ledbury Poetry Festival is not to be missed.

The Electronic Literature Organization site at **http://www.eliterature.org/** is a valuable resource with news and examples of all types of electronic literature. A new feature of the site is an ambitious database of available works. It's in beta-test as I write, and should be available by the time you read this. I can't always fit everything in, but let me know anyway, by way of:
peter@hphoward.demon.co.uk

PBS EXCLUSIVE BOOK SUPPLY SERVICE

Readers of *Poetry Review* can receive the UK-published books featured in the magazine post-free from the Poetry Book Society. If your local bookshop's idea of a poetry section is a shelf of Keats *Collected* and two tatty copies of *The Waste Land* this is what you've been waiting for! Call 020 8870 8403 between 9.30am and 5.30pm Mon-Fri to make your order, quoting "*Poetry Review*". All major credit/debit cards accepted, including Switch.

LETTERS

OXBOOK

Dear Peter,

I agree with much of what Anthony Thwaite says in his letter about my review of *The Oxford Book of English Verse* (Vol 90 No 1, p86). Still I can't help feeling that the 87 lines of his 'We are too many' poem is about 80 overlong, in the context of this anthology, and that Christopher Ricks's inclusion of it owes as much to donnish whimsy as it does to making a point about the mutability of fame and current reputations.

Thwaite also thinks that the editor's "crucial caveat" about not including poets who are "younger than I am" absolves him from my criticisms. To make Heaney the one exception to this rule, while ignoring Mahon, Harrison, Fisher, Fenton *et al* seems craven to me, a bow to fashion and the herd instinct – something critics and decent anthologists are supposed to combat.

I owe Professor Ricks himself an apology for foisting on him an "eighty-page essay on Geoffrey Hill's use of hyphens" which, as he points out (Vol 90 No 2, p110), is an exaggeration. I mistakenly conflated his two essays on Hill in *The Force of Poetry* (seventy pages in all), only one of which enters into the arcana of the hyphen. I admire Ricks's close-reading expertise. My beef was and is that his relish for nuance, indirection and dubious puns can become a means of not engaging with those substantive issues which go beyond verbal quibbling and Empsonian pyrotechnics. Compare and contrast Tom Paulin on Hill, for example, Hugh Kenner and Ted Hughes on Eliot, or Randall Jarrell on practically anybody.

As for the use of "Sir" This and "Lord" That on his Contents page, the point is surely that Henry Howard is (in Ricks's own words) "better-known"as the Earl of Surrey, just as John Wilmot is better-known as the Earl of Rochester. Does the addition of "Sir" add anything to the name-recognition of Betjeman and Empson? Surrey and Rochester lived in ages when royalist handles meant something. It's a minor point, and I don't want to flog it, but the English genius for mixing up art, "heritage" and flummery should be severely discouraged. All three are apt to be met with in Oxford anthologies.

Yours sincerely,

WILLIAM SCAMMELL

SOME CONTRIBUTORS

Gillian Allnutt's fifth collection, *Lintel,* will be published by Bloodaxe in 2001.

Connie Bensley's latest collection is *The Back and the Front of It* (Bloodaxe).

Ros Barber was shortlisted for the 1999 Geoffey Dearmer Prize.

Eleanor Cooke's *Secret Files* was published by Cape in 1994.

Andy Croft's *Letter to Randall Swingler* was published by Shoestring Press in 1999.

Alison Croggon was featured in 'The Republic of Sprawl' (PR, Vol 89 No 1, 1999).

Michael Donaghy's new collection *Conjure* is a PBS Choice.

Rose Flint had a Poetry Placement in a doctor's waiting room.

John Fuller's *Collected Poems* were published by Chatto in 1996.

Brian Henry's first collection, *Astronaut* (Arc) is on the Forward Prize shortlist; he is an editor of *Verse*.

Rita Ann Higgins' latest collection is *Sunny Side Plucked* (Bloodaxe, 1996).

Jane Holland's new collection is forthcoming from Bloodaxe.

Hugh Macpherson was shortlisted for the Geoffrey Dearmer Prize in 1999.

Roger McGough's latest collection is *The Way Things Are* (Penguin, 2000).

Justin Quinn's second collection, *Privacy,* was published by Carcanet in 1999.

Simon Rae won the 1999 Natonal Poetry Competition

Maurice Riordan's new collection, *Floods* (Faber), was published in September.

Vernon Scannell's *Views and Distances* was published by Enitharmon in April.

Ruth Sharman's first collection is *Birth of the Owl Butterflies* (Picador, 1997)

Penelope Shuttle's latest collection is *A Leaf Out of His Book* (Oxford Poets, 1999).

Stephen Troussé is the editor of *papercuts* magazine.

Sarah Wardle won the 1999 Geoffrey Dearmer Prize.

David Wheatley's first collection, *Thirst*, was published by Gallery. He is an editor of *Metre*.

John Hartley Williams' latest collection is *Canada* (1997).

CORRECTIONS

The third stanza of Jane Holland's poem, 'The Birth of The Medicine Man', unfortunately appeared incorrectly in the last issue (p.100). It should read:

When I was old enough to dream
I began to remember
how they took me
away from my family,
told me to run
and shot bullets of quartz crystal
after me. One entered
the white space of my head
and spoke to me.